Y0-BCW-671

FATHER
BISHOP

Founder OF THE
Glenmary Home Missioners

FATHER BISHOP

FOUNDER OF THE
GLENMARY HOME MISSIONERS

Herman W. Santen

CATHOLIC LIFE PUBLICATIONS
BRUCE PRESS • MILWAUKEE

and

THE GLENMARY HOME MISSIONERS
GLENDALE, OHIO

NIHIL OBSTAT:

CARL R. STEINBICKER, S.T.D.
Censor librorum

IMPRIMATUR:

✠ PAUL F. LEIBOLD, V.G.
The Archdiocese of Cincinnati
October 7, 1960

WHEN a talented man has a special job that needs doing, he carefully selects his tools and gets to work.

In much the same way, when almighty God, in His omniscient Providence, wants to take care of some problem down here on earth, He selects His tool for the work and so provides that the job can be accomplished. Now God's tools are very often human beings. If the person He selects happens to be somewhat imperfect, the skill and grace of the divine Artisan can make up for what is lacking in man.

Imperfect man, divinely handled, has often accomplished what seemed to be impossible. Saints are quick to recognize their own limitations and imperfections, but God does the sanctifying, and He is the One who oversees the work He wants performed. God knows what He is doing when He chooses His tool for a certain task.

When Arianism grew strong in opposition to the truths of the Creed, along came an Athanasius from Alexandria reaffirming to the world Christ's Divinity. As a saintly patriarch, he had to spend seventeen years in banishment but, undismayed, he won over many of the Arians through kindness and calm reasoning. Whenever a weakening Catholic Europe needed rebuilding, along came a Benedict, a Dominic, a Francis, or an Ignatius. When France was fast losing its religious fervor at the time of Bonaparte, God "graced" a Curé d'Ars to help the Faith of thousands upon thousands.

We can also believe that God "hand-picked" Father Bishop for the work of founding a society that is to help take care of a big problem facing the Church in America today.

The Church in America graduated from the "missionary" status several generations ago. Quickly, she has learned to stand on her own feet! She has also learned that she must share some of the burden of missionizing other parts of the world. This she actually has begun to do remarkably well, thus demonstrating her Catholicity even while maturing and gaining strength to walk unassisted.

But no one would foolishly believe that simply because America is sending missioners into other lands, she no longer has mission problems at home. Most of the American hierarchy know our country so well that they not only encourage, but also lend a helpful hand to individuals and societies at work in the home missions. The 700 counties and 60,000 cities, towns, and hamlets that are found priestless and churchless cause real concern to many of our fellow churchmen. Much of rural America is indifferent to Christianity; much of it is fast becoming out and out pagan.

Today, when immigration is practically at a standstill, the Church no longer has great increases in numbers and percentages of population from Catholic Europe; on the contrary, the vast majority of the people now coming into our big cities from rural America are not Catholics.

Father William Howard Bishop and a few of his contemporaries learned of this problem. As country pastor and president for five consecutive years of the National Catholic Rural Life Conference, he had ample opportunity for studying every statistic and other available knowledge about the Church in rural America. Father Bishop saw the dangerous implication of the non-ending stream of non-Catholics pouring into our city parishes. Others must see the importance of it, too, and something must be done about it right away.

Father Bishop talked and wrote articles proposing a solution to the problem until finally one day he was invited by the Archbishop of Cincinnati to come to the Archdiocese. Here, sympathetic souls could help his plan take shape.

Many of the clergy and lay folk saw the timely importance of his plan of starting a society of secular priests which would specialize in the one big job of bringing the Catholic Faith to the non-Catholics of No Priest Land, U.S.A.

Fortunately for the success of the Society, some of the oldest of Cincinnati's Catholic families befriended Father Bishop. The first young apostles to join him introduced him to the Harry Santens, the Mayor Al Cashs, the Earls, the Walter Herschedes and the Walter Grotes, the various Albers families, the Gus Longs, the William Dolles, the John Glasers, the Henry Kenneys and the Dan Heekins, the Malones, the Castellinis, the Kytes, Twomeys, Favrets, the Raymond Buses, the Williams, and Leis, Doctors Hutzelman, Goldcamp, Schrimpf, Schlueter, Dornheggen, and their families. All of them joined forces, along with the Archdiocese and friends beyond, to help this tottering young Society start its work in the vast mission areas.

Father Bishop more than once remarked to his young confreres about the extraordinarily fine families of Cincinnati. Among them, he had some very close friends. Precisely because of his twenty-year intimate association with the Santens, I have asked Harry Santen to write the first biography of our beloved founder. Other biographies might be written later, but this one will be helpful to other writings about Father Bishop and the Glenmary Home Missioners.

Mr. Santen is a successful Catholic lawyer. He is presently practicing with his two sons. The fact that he is a good lawyer assures us of a sincerity and accuracy in his writings. The book is factual, allowing neither minimizing nor exaggeration. Here at Glenmary, we think his book a very good biography of our founder as seen through the eyes of a Catholic layman, a close friend, who shared with Father Bishop much of that which could be rightfully shared.

Father Bishop kept a daily diary. After Father's death, Mr. Santen was permitted access to this diary and other important letters and papers pertinent to the writing of a good biography. You will not only find "interesting reading" but also learn much about the man and the priest, Father Bishop. As the pages unfold, you may also see why almighty God "hand-picked" Father Bishop to help the Church in America meet a problem that must be solved as quickly and as effectually as possible. Souls are at stake!

> Very Rev. Clement F. Borchers
> *Superior General*
> *Glenmary Home Missioners*

Reverend William Howard Bishop

Reverend Dear Father:

I am happy to welcome you to the Archdiocese of Cincinnati. The Archbishop of Baltimore, recognizing the thoughtful and prayerful years through which you have passed in preparing for a work which I hope will be abundantly blessed by God, has granted you an indefinite leave of absence.

I ask you to go to the historic section of Brown County and to take charge, temporarily, of St. Martin Parish. I have recommended your proposed home mission society to the priests of the archdiocese assembled in retreat, asking their prayers and urging them to favor you and your companions, especially during the first struggling period of organization.

It is important that an episcopal board be formed, which you can consult whenever you need the direction of the Church and which will enable you to profit by the missionary experience of many dioceses. I have already asked several bishops to serve on this board. They have gladly consented to serve.

Asking God to bless you and your work, and trusting that Cincinnati will give to you some of its best men, because the mission field should have the best, I am

Faithfully yours in Christ,

✠ JOHN T. McNICHOLAS
Archbishop of Cincinnati

Very Reverend William Howard Bishop

My dear Father Bishop:

I thank you for your letter in which you tell me of the progress which you are making in your holy enterprise to carry on a priestly apostolate on the countryside.

From the beginning of your undertaking I have followed your work with interest and expectancy. There is a characteristic of the Mission of Christ which is frequently overlooked and it comes from His sane realism. Other teachers, great in talents and exalted in ideals, have had the touch of the unrealistic about their work. "He knew what is in man." Now the Apostolate must catch this utter realism of the Master. In the light of it we see that its outstanding problem in the United States is a rural problem. I do not refer merely to the socio-christian rural problem which is happily engaging the attention of many good priests and laymen but to the need of recognizing that the future growth of the Church and even holding its own in the United States depends on our exhibiting the spectacle of the Church on the countryside in this day. You have delineated this problem and with a reasoned zeal are attacking it. Quite naturally your work is engaging the attention and arousing the hopes of the many who are familiar with it,

I wish you continued success and every news item which will tell of your progress will be a consolation to me.

Sincerely yours in Christ,

✠ SAMUEL A. STRITCH
Archbishop of Milwaukee

Reverend William Howard Bishop

Dear Father Bishop:

The news that you are seeking to inaugurate a movement to help the rural missions has not come to me as a complete surprise, but rather as a confirmation of long cherished hope. The other sheep of our own country have been calling for missionaries for a century. A glorious field of apostolic labor is waiting. If your enterprise proves to be the Providential means designed by Almighty God to answer this call and staff this field, surely the Church of America will rejoice.

Your movement holds a peculiar interest for me and for all at Maryknoll, inasmuch as it tends to emphasize a theory held strongly by our beloved founders. When Bishop James Anthony Walsh and Father Price inaugurated their venture in fields afar, they had no notion of thereby robbing the fields at home. They held on the other hand that the expansion of charity involved in foreign missions could not fail to stimulate and benefit the home missions. They prophesied that the foreign effort, by a natural reaction (and also supernatural), would witness an increase of zeal for the home effort. Father Price, particularly, as you know, had already spent a lifetime in the home mission work before he left it to join in founding Maryknoll. He did not transfer his affections. He regarded his new work, not as an abandonment of the home missions which he loved, but rather as an act of logical continuation that could not fail to benefit them in even greater degree. Your generous appraisal of his North Carolina apostolate as a forerunner of your own is gratefully appreciated by us.

I might add that it was the belief of Bishop Walsh, often expressed at Maryknoll, that the home mission problem would eventually be solved by a special organization fitted for the task. It is a work to be done by priests, and its success will lie in an organization that can supply and guarantee the proper preliminary training and the proper lifetime care of the priests who perform it.

May the blessing of God rest on your zealous enterprise. Your beginnings will probably be humble and difficult, but all works of God look for head winds at the start. If it attains its objective of filling our neglected countryside with ardent and persevering apostles, it will be worth all it costs.

With best wishes, dear Father Bishop, and with union of prayers, I am,

Sincerely yours in Christ,

✠ James E. Walsh
Superior General

Reverend William Howard Bishop

Dear Father:

As a member of the American Board of Catholic Missions, I have had an unusual opportunity to become familiar with the mission needs under the American Flag, and have often wished that there would be inaugurated and developed a Society of priests who would devote their lives to the service of scattered Catholics, to the reclamation of the lapsed Catholics, and to the evangelization of non-Catholics resident in the same wide area.

I am glad that you contemplate launching an undertaking designed to meet these very urgent needs, and I pray that Almighty God may richly bless and prosper your enterprise.

Sincerely in Christ,

✠ John F. Noll
Bishop of Fort Wayne

Segneteria di Stato
       Di
   Sua Santita
   No. 299697/SA

                                    Vatican City, July 24, 1953

The Glenmary Home Missioners
Very Reverend Raphael A. Sourd, Vicar General
Glendale, Ohio

Very Reverend and dear Father Sourd:

It is my revered duty to convey in the name of the Holy Father, to you and to the members of the Community of the Glenmary Missioners this expression of sincere regret and prayerful sympathy at the loss so recently sustained in the death of your saintly founder and first Superior General, the Very Reverend Father W. Howard Bishop.

The example of his holy life and his zeal in founding this work so important for the advancement of the Church in those parts of the United States where the fewness of the Catholic faithful constitute an area of truly missionary endeavor, will have left its impress on all those who have dedicated themselves to his ideal and will continue to inspire them in being faithful to its accomplishment.

As a token of these sentiments and in pledge of paternal interest in your work His Holiness imparts to you and to all your associates among the Glenmary Missioners His Apostolic Benediction.

With my personal sympathy and prayerful regard, I am,

                              Sincerely yours in Christ,

                              ✠ J. B. MONTINI
                                 Prosecr.

FATHER
BISHOP

Founder OF THE
Glenmary Home Missioners

CHAPTER 1

AT THE top of the ramp, opening into the waiting room of the railroad depot in Cincinnati, Ohio, Father W. Howard Bishop stopped for a moment and in a soft Maryland drawl thanked the porter who carried his bag. He was a stranger in this Midwestern city. The murals of colored mosaics along the wall, showing the farmer and the backwoodsman in life size, brought his mind directly to the sheaf of papers he carried in his brief case. It was a happy omen that here in the terminal depot of Cincinnati an artist had idealized the frontiersman and here in the same depot was a priest who sought to found a Society to extend the Catholic way of life from its city strongholds to the frontiers of rural America.

Cincinnati was perhaps not the end of his dream. He had visited many dioceses — Chicago, New York, Baltimore, Philadelphia — to no avail, but many remained. It was not in his nature to admit defeat; nor was he discouraged. Cincinnati might well be the cradle city of the Society he hoped to found. He had spread out those papers in his brief case on many a conference table, and many Catholic Bishops had listened attentively. All recognized the importance of a planned, but peaceful, invasion of the rural counties of America, where there were no resident priests. Invasion, of course, was a word Father Bishop never used. It connotes an unwelcome visit.

1

But Father Bishop knew that souls in rural America awaited the Church with open arms. To him the welcome sign was evident. Unfortunately, the masses of city dwellers had exhausted the organized strength of the Catholic hierarchy and only sporadic efforts remained for the rural heart and sinew of the nation. With conditions as they were, a Catholic priest appointed by his Bishop to a poor rural area could usually not remain there long enough to make the Church and school the heart center of a Catholic community.

Father Bishop's plan provided for a society of priests, Brothers and Sisters, trained to live in the priestless counties of rural America, happy to say Mass for ten Catholics or less, who would in time be the core of a parish school and church. His men and women would gain no recognition in cities, although the product of their work, trained intelligent Catholic rural dwellers, might well migrate to the crowded centers, bringing to the city a renewed moral vitality.

Father Bishop found no opposition from the prelates with whom he discussed his plans. But only Archbishop Murray of St. Paul had agreed to sponsor him, and then only if Cincinnati would not do so. Cincinnati, the Archbishop thought, was an ideal location to start a Society which would work in the South and West, but would draw vocations from the more strongly Catholic North and East.

As a delegate to the Catholic Rural Life Conference, this Maryland priest had stressed at a recent meeting in St. Louis the expansion of Catholicity on the land. Among those present were Bishop Karl J. Alter of Toledo, who later became Archbishop of Cincinnati. From St. Louis, Father Bishop had gone up to Chicago and then to St. Paul to visit the Ordinaries, and finally down to Cincinnati on the off chance of seeing His Excellency, John T. McNicholas, Archbishop of Cincinnati.

To him he carried a letter of introduction from the late Bishop Ireton of Richmond, Virginia.

The Archbishop of Cincinnati was not a stranger to Father Bishop. At meetings of the National Catholic Rural Life Conference, Father Bishop had appraised him as a fearless prelate, as an idealist who transmuted into reality ideas about which others only talked.

So it was on Saturday, April 17, 1937, that Father Bishop, a parish priest of Clarksville, Maryland, fifty-one years of age, came to Cincinnati. At 7:30 A.M. the city was awakening to a spring morning. Slowly along the wide parkway moved the street railway bus, in which he rode to the chancery offices. This was a time for thought. Would the Archbishop file the dream away as a plan for the future? Or would he say with characteristic energy: "Go to your priest-neglected land and know that in my diocese you may recruit, you may build, and I will stand by you"? Today might give the answer.

The Archbishop was a Dominican, a member of one of the oldest orders of the Church, the Order of Preachers. Would he consider it presumptuous that a priest of his generation sought to found a new Society? Maryknoll, a Society of secular priests founded in the United States to do missionary work in pagan countries, was comparatively young and Bishop Walsh, its Superior, was a close friend of Archbishop McNicholas. Perhaps at one time or another the Maryknoller had said to His Excellency, as he said to Father Bishop: "A society such as you propose should have been founded fifty years ago."

At Eighth and Walnut Streets he left the bus and entered the Chancery offices. Bishop Albers, the Auxiliary of the Archdiocese, and the Chancellor, Monsignor Thill, welcomed him.

In the afternoon the critical moment arrived. Father Bishop sat with the Archbishop in his study. Laying his missionary map on the table, Father Bishop pointed out that one third of the three thousand counties in the nation were without resident priests. These counties he had colored in black. He traced the dark area as it thickened in the southland from the Atlantic to the Mississippi and thence west into New Mexico, and northeast into Colorado, Utah, and Idaho. In every other state he pointed to a sprinkling of black, except the New England States and New York, New Jersey, Delaware, Wisconsin, and Arizona. In these black areas, he said, large families were plentiful and the birth rate was supplying both rural and urban sections with whatever increases they enjoyed in native born population. Here little or no missionary labors had been expended.

"If that situation is not corrected," Father Bishop predicted, "the future will bring a gradual decline of Catholic strength in the urban centers, which are presently the strongholds of Catholicity in America, because there will be no compensating gains from the country where the Church is the weakest. But if we throw a proportionately strong and persevering missionary offensive into the country, we shall by that single strategy strengthen the Church's stand both rurally and in the cities."

"If we grant the vast importance and extent of the rural mission field," he argued, "then we must concede that isolated missionary forays will not win the battle. Specialized training is necessary and there must be a continuity and a persistence through succeeding generations of the objectives that we seek. Logically, I find no solution but a separate society of secular priests with its own Superior and Rule to lead the way, to develop a missionary technique and to supply methods and other helps to diocesan priests not specially trained for this work."

"As you will note from this sketchy map," he continued, "Cincinnati is just to the north of the blackest areas. It is an ideal place in which to start the Missionary Society I propose."

The Archbishop was deeply interested. He asked: "How do you answer a bishop who suggests he can recruit his own diocesan priests, to man his own rural parishes and perhaps even create new ones?"

Father Bishop replied: "Your Grace, I am a rural pastor. Many times my own Archbishop Curley of Baltimore suggested that I move to other more important parishes in his Archdiocese. Fortunately, I was able to persuade him that I might be of little use in working with the masses of a big city parish. Without a Society your men must be vowed to the rural apostolate, and not for a short time until they can become pastors of your city parishes, but for all of their priestly lives. To carry out their mission priests must go to the rural parishes, prepared and ready to remain in the country; they must take root there. That would necessitate a special group, completely cut off from any ambitions to move to the city. To accomplish this you would in effect be organizing a society, but one limited to your own needs. I submit to Your Grace that the problem is in and for all America. It is not limited to one diocese."

The Archbishop asked many more questions; he proposed many difficulties. The afternoon wore away. At dinner the discussion was continued. Later the die was cast. The Society of the Home Missions could organize and build in the city of Cincinnati under the direction of the Archbishop until such time as it could justify itself as a diocesan religious society.

Father Bishop noted in his diary certain requirements. Archbishop Curley of Baltimore had to release him from that diocese. Archbishop McNicholas must know in detail the steps the priest proposed to take in organizing his Society. Certain canonical questions concerning the responsibility and authority of the Archbishop of Cincinnati had to be discussed with the Canonists of the Archdiocese. To Father Bishop these were minor details.

In heavy black ink, aside from every other comment, Father Bishop noted in his diary: "SATURDAY, APRIL 17, 1937, THE ARCHBISHOP OF CINCINNATI AGREES TO HEADQUARTER MY SOCIETY."

CHAPTER 2

MANY miles stretch between Cincinnati and Wilmington, North Carolina, where Father Bishop's father was born. It is a state where the English-speaking stock is almost untouched by foreign elements. On the indented Atlantic seacoast, Wilmington early became an important seaport, connecting the new world with its motherland, England. In the early 1800's here came Henry Morrell Bishop on an English ship. He settled and married Sarah Ann Shaler, whose father, Morgan Shaler, had fought in the War of Independence.

Their son was Francis Besant Bishop, born in 1852. Few Catholics lived in Wilmington, but the Faith was kept alive in the small church and school of St. Thomas, the Apostle. The Bishop family were Episcopalians, as was Alfred Lanier Price, the editor of the Wilmington *Daily Journal*. It is interesting to note that Alfred Price was received into the Catholic Church on Christmas Day, 1866, and that his son, Thomas Frederick Price, the co-founder of Maryknoll, became a home missioner in North Carolina, and finally a foreign missioner in China, where he died.

Two years after that Christmas Day, 1868, when the father of Howard Bishop was fifteen years old, Alfred Price, the convert, welcomed to Washington the youngest Catholic Bishop in the United States, James Gibbons, who was installed in St. Thomas Church as the Vicar Apostolic of North Carolina.

At his consecration, Father Thomas Foley, later Bishop of Chicago at the time of the great fire, said: "And you, Right Reverend Sir, are to go to the large state of North Carolina. It appalls one to think of a state of nearly a million inhabitants with but few altars and one or two priests to minister to them."

Over the colonial years Catholics had moved in and out of North Carolina, but the lack of priests and churches caused their faith to wane and be swallowed in the social and business life of a Protestant community. Even in Wilmington, the Church of St. Thomas the Apostle was not built until the summer of 1847.

In 1868 when Bishop Gibbons, later the first American Cardinal, came to North Carolina to start his apostolic labors, the city of Wilmington was impoverished, as were the Bishops. The Civil War had ended, bringing in its wake carpetbaggers who flocked to the city. Young Francis Bishop had to work in a hardware store, reading when he could and fostering the thought of studying medicine.

A Catholic group led by Alfred Price, editor of the only Wilmington newspaper, centered its activities around St. Thomas Church. Undoubtedly, it was in this group that Francis Bishop met his future wife, Ella Knowles, who lived at Fayetteville, perhaps forty miles west of Wilmington on the Cape Fear River. Educated in a Convent at Richmond, Virginia, she was an ardent Catholic. To attend Mass, she had to travel the forty miles to Wilmington as there was no church in Fayetteville. In his diary, Bishop Gibbons recalls that at least once he said Mass in Fayetteville at a Catholic home.

With the help of Dr. Norcum, a physician in Wilmington, and Thomas P. Howard, a friend of the family, for whom Father Bishop was named, young Francis Bishop studied medicine. He was a fledgling doctor in 1875 when he married

Ella Knowles, promising that his children would be baptized and raised as Catholics.

In 1876, when Dr. Bishop was twenty-three years old, his first child was born, Mary Edna. The family grew. Their first son was born two years later, John Knowles Bishop; the second daughter, Frances, in 1880, and in 1882 the fourth child, Grace.

Sometime in that period Dr. Bishop became a Catholic. The prayers of his wife, Ella, were answered. Dr. Bishop spent hours in Baltimore in the hospitals seeking the latest results of medical research. He knew and admired Bishop Gibbons, then the Primate of Baltimore. Father Bishop later said his father's admiration for His Excellency furnished the final thrust that led him into the Catholic fold.

It was at this time in 1883 that Dr. Francis Bishop decided to take his family to Washington, the nation's capital. He was fortunate in finding a home to rent on Washington Circle at 23rd Street off Pennsylvania Avenue.

The capital was still a sleepy southern city; the houses were small, close together, each with a clean-swept stone stoop. From Washington Circle one could see the white, unfinished shaft of the Washington Monument to be completed a year later. The front room, which opened abruptly from the stone stoop, was the doctor's office. Here his patients came, at first a mere trickle, but later, as his ability was recognized, they crowded the cane-seated chairs along the wall.

Doctor Bishop moved a year later to the permanent home at 1913 "I" Street. Here was born William Howard Bishop on December 19, 1886. His sister, Mary Edna, then nine years old, welcomed him. To her he was a live doll to be petted and pampered. To his brother John, age seven, he was a demanding creature who monopolized his mother's attention; and to Frances and Grace, his two infant sisters, ages five and three, he was a fragile toy, whom they could hardly touch without a word of restraint from their oldest sister, Edna. Over the household rested the necessity of quiet play, for their father, the doctor, used the front room as his surgery. Only in the mornings when the good doctor visited his patients could the children romp.

As they grew older the children of Doctor Bishop went to Force Public School. On Saturday mornings a nun gave them religious instructions at the Parish Hall of St. Stephen's Church. On Sunday afternoons before Vespers they attended a Sunday School conducted by the parish priest. Throughout his life Father Bishop urged the need of a Catholic school for Catholic children. From his own experience he realized the importance of the daily routine of prayer and the deep brand left upon his soul by the daily repetition of Catholic precepts.

When Howard Bishop was twelve years old, a mild cold persisted until he was taken to the hospital, burning with fever. The doctors diagnosed pneumonia. Day after day his temperature rose and the crisis approached. His mother promised Our Lady that if he lived she would work and pray that he might one day offer Mass at her altar. The boy recovered, but convalescence was long and tedious. Two years of schooling were missed. At some time during this period he heard his mother repeat her promise to a neighbor. Until he registered at the seminary, he fought against what he imagined to be a gift of his life without his own full consent.

At fifteen, Howard Bishop began his high school years at Central Washington High School. His younger brother, Harry, who later became a doctor, was his fellow student. Unlike Harry Bishop who excelled at intramural sports, Howard, because of his health, had to find other activities. In one of his early projects, he founded a neighborhood newspaper, obtaining ads from tradesmen in the vicinity and getting the weekly news sheet printed by a friendly printer. Throughout his life, Father Bishop had a flair for journalism. He learned early that the printed word is the finest medium for the widespread distribution of thoughts and ideas. Naturally, he gravitated to the Central High monthly called "The Review." He became its editor, specializing even at that age in writing editorials, commenting on school policies, urging unity and participation in school activities.

William Howard Bishop graduated from Central High School in 1906. He was the editor of "The Brecky C," published by the graduating class. His photograph in the annual was that of a young man with an intelligent face, serious perhaps, but unmistakably with a sense of humor. His contemporaries described him in "The Brecky C" as a born politician and proofreader, possessing a terrible temper, but controlled by a sweet disposition and an "excellent appetite." The latter remark was intended to be humorous as young Bishop was rather thin, belying any tendency to overeating.

If at twenty years of age Howard Bishop had a desire to become a priest, he did not indicate it to his family. Unquestionably, however, he was developing his spiritual life. He confined his reading to works of nonfiction, finding an emotional outlet in the poems of Keats and Shelley. Introspectively, he found in his Catholic Faith a sure guide to the solution of problems presented in the books he read. At odd times, he dropped into one or other of the many churches in Washington and lost himself in mental conversation with his very personal God. To his family he was a dreamer. Apparently, he was searching for a goal in life, but what form it would take was problematical. Unfortunately, he met few priests to guide him. His father, deep in his own study of electrotherapy, was of little help. His brother John, an artist, and also characterized as a dreamer, was more interested in the material beauty of life than in its spiritual significance. Of one thing Howard Bishop was certain. He, himself, had too little knowledge to make a decision for his own future. He required further study.

In the fall of 1906 he registered at Harvard University. His roommate was John Priest, who had graduated with him from Central High School. Humorously, Father Bishop remarked later:

"We had the entire hierarchy on our floor. I was a Bishop, Jack a Priest, and down the hall lived Bill Pope."

Dr. Charles William Elliott was then completing his thirty-seventh year as President of Harvard University. Its deeply conservative faculty had given way to a group of modern educators. The compulsory religious worship, a relic of John Harvard, its Puritan founder, had long been abolished. A Catholic undergraduate, while still somewhat of a rarity, met on equal terms non-Catholic students who welcomed religious discussions. Howard Bishop did not avoid them.

In his Freshman and Sophomore years he studied English, History, Psychology, and Mathematics. The reading of poetry was a relaxation. In the harsh New England winters periodic colds hindered his studies. Added to this susceptibility, a curvature of the spine developed, a bothersome affliction that he bore until the end of his life.

In the summer of 1908, Howard Bishop sold maps along the eastern coast for Underwood and Underwood of New York. His plan was to return to Harvard in the fall, better prepared financially and physically to complete his studies. The summer lengthened into fall, and with his health no better, he decided to wait a full year before resuming his studies. In the mean-

time, he had never ceased to stop in churches in every town
he visited. Before the altar of Our Lady he would lose himself
in meditation.

The summer of 1909 was the turning point of his life.
Gradually he had become aware that he could not find peace
of soul in the material world. What inner spiritual conflict
he had was not disclosed. It is certain that never did he think
of adopting the medical profession of his father. He decided
to apply for admission to St. Charles's Seminary in Baltimore,
Maryland. He was twenty-four years of age, a dreamer, but
one who, his friends said, could make a quick decision. He
was totally unaware of the requirements the Church exacts
of those who would enter the priesthood. Yet he knew that
he would have to convince someone in authority of the reality
and permanency of his resolve. And so he called on James
Cardinal Gibbons, the Archbishop of Baltimore, who suggested
that he consult his pastor at St. Stephen's Church, and if he
approved, enter a month's retreat at the Trappist Monastery
in Providence, Rhode Island. The proper approach, of course,
was to have seen his pastor before consulting the Archbishop.
But we must remember that Howard Bishop had attended
public schools all his life, and knew few priests to advise him.
In the monastery he found the spiritual counsel he needed.
Above all he had to yield his will to that of the Superior. His
studies had to conform to the pattern set by the Church. Prayer,
meditation, and reflection confirmed his resolution. He was
ready to begin his quest for the Holy Grail.

In the autumn of 1909 he presented himself to St. Mary's
Seminary in Baltimore, founded by the Sulpicians after their
expulsion from France. He was alone, dressed in the gray suit
in which he had traveled the New England States selling road

maps. In his later years he recalled, with a twinkle in his eye, that the Sulpician Rector had suggested a black suit was more suitable for a seminarian.

The years at the seminary passed quickly, filled as they were with prayer, meditation, and study. In his second year, he became a Bachelor of Arts, and in his third year a Master of Arts. The minor orders of Porter, Lector, Exorcist, Acolyte, and Subdeacon followed in the usual sequence, and in 1914 on May 20 he received the Diaconate at the hands of Bishop Corrigan, rector of the Catholic University at Washington.

Howard Bishop had not yet attained the knowledge he desired. With the consent of the Archbishop, he applied to the rector of the Catholic University for admission as a student in the School of Philosophy. He had every intention of qualifying as a teacher in the University.

Events, however, were moving rapidly. World War I had made a battleground of Europe, with England, France, and Germany locked in trench warfare. The world had embarked on a course, the end of which no one could foresee. For fifty years bands had not played martial music to stir the desire for adventure, nor had the measured military tread of soldiers been heard on Washington's wide Pennsylvania Avenue. The clamor of the outside world was heard in the halls of philosophy. From time to time, Howard Bishop felt an urge to participate in the open market place, not in its material, but in its spiritual problems. However, he remained an alert student. According to the records of the University his average in philosophy was one hundred for the second semester of the scholastic year, 1914–1915, and for the previous semester, ninety-nine.

CHAPTER 3

ON MARCH 27, 1915, in the Chapel of Caldwell Hall at the Catholic University Howard Bishop heard the words of Bishop Shahan: "Thou art a priest forever." His mother was the first to kiss his upturned palms. His father knelt to receive his blessing.

On a later occasion, in a talk to scholastics in his own Society, he re-iterated a truth which was a loadstone of his character. He said: "Not we — but the priesthood is great. It is providential that we do not realize how unworthy of the priesthood we are. St. Francis of Assisi realized too well its greatness, and so he could not bring himself to accept the honor, but remained a deacon until he died. To be a priest is to be the teacher and exemplar of Christian living. The honors of the priesthood must be for those of great humility."

On Easter Sunday Father Bishop sang his First Solemn High Mass at the Church of St. James in West Falls, Virginia. His first assignment was a week-end appointment as assistant to Father Bart, pastor of St. Teresa's Church in Anacostia, a suburb of Washington. There he preached his first sermon, using as his text the Gospel of the Good Shepherd. In a pew near the front of the Church sat his mother and father.

In June at the completion of a year at the Catholic University, he was sent to North Cliff, Maryland, as chaplain of the Convent of Villa Maria. The nuns externally were not of a pattern, but all walked softly through the corridors like the gentle motion of draperies in a light wind. All were kindly, considerate, and generous to the young priest. In his talk on his last Sunday with them he said that the inspiration of their lives was a sermon he could never forget.

On August 1, 1915, he definitely abandoned his hope of teaching when he received the Archbishop's appointment as curate to Father Craig at the Shrine of the Sacred Heart in Mt. Washington, a suburb of Baltimore, Maryland.

He was little prepared for his first parish. An idealist and a dreamer, he had thought of a parish as a pool of good Catholic folk into which he would toss some of the ideas he had dreamed about and watch the ripples spread until they touched a whole sea of humanity. What he found was that parishes, like people, require food and housing; need a thousand and one material things. The young curate wondered where, in this mass of routine tasks to be done by the clock, was there room for the mystical and the spiritual. Experience was lacking of the minutiae of a parish priest. He had chosen his vocation from the high plane of an intellectual. At the seminary and at the Catholic University his professors had filled his days with theological and philosophical truths which, although present in every moment's task, obscured the business of just living by their very brilliance. He knew from his theology that it was his task to point out that "just living" in accordance with easily followed moral principles must lead to God, but it was difficult to recognize the application of this truth to the importance of Sunday collections, or the necessity of church social affairs where the young curate found himself ill at ease. It was a confusing transition period.

His pastor, Father Craig, a tried and experienced priest, had been brought here a short time before to erect a new church, and his reputation as a builder had preceded him. The ease with which he obtained subscriptions for the new edifice amazed his young curate, whose timidity in asking for donations sometimes exasperated his superior; but Father Bishop learned rapidly. He was a dreamer, but he was determined to build dreams into reality. He saw Father Craig stir a slumbering parish into active life. A rectory across the street was renovated. In it the young priest had a small but well furnished room with ample space for his books, which he found little time to read. A newly recruited group of altar boys was placed under his direction. The annual lawn fete required time. The spiritual care of the good sisters at Mount St. Agnes was entrusted to him. They mothered the young curate, and sometimes exasperated him by their gratuitous advice on just how he should preach and the topics of his sermons.

So a month passed, and in September he learned that his spine required imprisonment in a straight jacket for a year or more if the daily pain was to be eliminated. Years later the brace was discarded, but throughout his life the pain persisted. It was characteristic of the man that he never permitted physical pain to interfere with the work he demanded of himself. Nor did he ever lose the gentleness and refinement of an educated southern gentleman.

As the assistant to the pastor, he had the duty of taking the census. He found the work fascinating. Necessarily, he learned the problems of the wage earners and of the wealthier members of his parish. In the encyclicals of Pope Leo XIII, on Capital and Labor, he found the modern Catholic approach to these social problems.

March 27, 1916 was a happy day. Father Bishop wrote in his diary: "One year ago today I was ordained by Bishop Shahan in the Chapel at Caldwell Hall, Catholic University,

Washington. The good Sisters at the Convent had special flowers and music for my Mass. They prayed for me and all the girls and Sisters offered up their Communions. At the school, the children came in their best clothes and presented to me a bouquet of carnations — and another bouquet, a spiritual one of their prayers and Communions. What gift could be better?"

A month later, his father, Doctor Bishop, died at the age of sixty-three. He was buried from St. Stephen's Church with his son offering a Solemn Requiem High Mass. Among the mourners was Chief Justice White of the United States Supreme Court, a stanch Catholic, and his father's friend.

The routine life of a curate continued — daily Mass at 7, confessions on Saturday, sick calls, classes in the school, marriages. Interspersed were calls on his family and his friends. He visited his mother often, spending the night at her home, accepting the care she lavished upon him. Father Bishop's mother was shy and sensitive. At this period of his life he, too, was easily hurt. It led him, perhaps, to greater introspection, developing in him a deeper spiritual understanding. On January 1, 1917 he wrote in his diary:

"RESOLUTION

"I will endeavor by careful study of liturgy to make the Mass my chief preoccupation and care, the center of my religious life. I will preach frequently on the different phases of the sublime Sacrifice; this with the help of Almighty God and His Divine Son, whom it is my privilege to receive and offer up daily."

His Excellency,
Most Rev. John T. McNicholas, O.P.
Cincinnati, Ohio, Summer, 1952.

The Very Reverend William Howard Bishop, founder of
The Glenmary Home Missioners. This photo was taken in
1950 in the old farmhouse headquarters at Glendale, Ohio.

Eleanor Knowles Bishop, mother of Glenmary's founder, who promised him to God as a priest on condition of his recovery from an early illness.

As a student, Howard Bishop was editor of his high school literary review in Washington, D. C. Soon after this photo was taken he entered Harvard College.

Just two years after ordination Father Bishop was made country pastor of St. Louis Church, Clarksville, Md.

An early catechism class at Clarksville, Md.

A used truck served as school bus for Father Bishop's rural school, a novel experiment in his day.

In the summer of 1939, Father Bishop was joined by Father Raphael Sourd in a tent-preaching campaign. Father Sourd dedicated his life to the work at this time.

Open-air Talks to the People

on

The Catholic Church

and Her Teachings

With Pictures and Lectures on the Life of Jesus Christ

REV. RAPHAEL A. SOURD

REV. W. HOWARD BISHOP

Six Successive Evenings at 8 O'clock

Monday, July 17th to Saturday, July 22nd

Court House Square

West Union, Ohio

MONDAY, July 17—God and Man
TUESDAY, July 18—Christ and His Church
WEDNESDAY, July 19—The Church and the Bible

THURSDAY, July 20—The Forgiveness of Sin
FRIDAY, July 21—The Mass
SATURDAY, July 22—Mary, the Mother of Christ

Questions about the Catholic Church will be cheerfully answered

EVERYBODY WELCOME

No Charges   No Collections

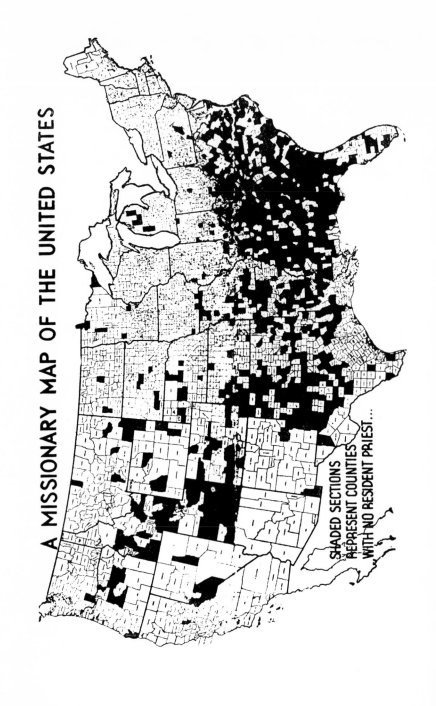

A MISSIONARY MAP OF THE UNITED STATES

SHADED SECTIONS
REPRESENT COUNTIES
WITH NO RESIDENT PRIEST...

The outdoor preaching on West Union's Court House Square developed into well-organized tent campaigns which moved through all of the Southland. It could boast of a highly skilled gospel harmony quartet, excellent religious movies, large crowds, and, in many cases, the beginning of new parishes.

The Chapel of the American Martyrs brought their first glimpse of a Catholic church to thousands in the southern Appalachian Mountains between 1940 and 1946. It was abandoned in favor of tent preaching.

St. Anne Church, Buena Vista, the first of many mission chapels constructed by Father Bishop's new mission society.

On frequent forays into the isolated country shown in black on the No-Priest-Land map, Father Bishop personally photographed the people and their way of life to focus America's attention on this problem through the pages of *Glenmary's Challenge*. The gentleman pictured lived in the mountains of eastern Kentucky.

His Holiness, Pope Pius XII.

The Glenmary Sisters, a co-operating Society, was organized in 1941. By 1960 over 100 young women had dedicated their lives to No-Priest-Land. This photograph was made in the summer of 1954.

In the spring of 1951 Father Bishop broke ground for the south wing of Our Lady of the Fields Seminary.

One of the last photographs made of Father Bishop shows him with the first Chapter which adopted the Glenmary Constitution in the summer of 1951. One year later Father Bishop completed a period of six months as a novice in his own Society.

The architect's drawing for Our Lady of the Fields Seminary and headquarters of the Society at Glendale, Ohio. The southern colonial architecture reflects the aim of the society to work among the poor in No-Priest-Land counties which are most numerous in the Southeast.

No Priest Land U.S.A.

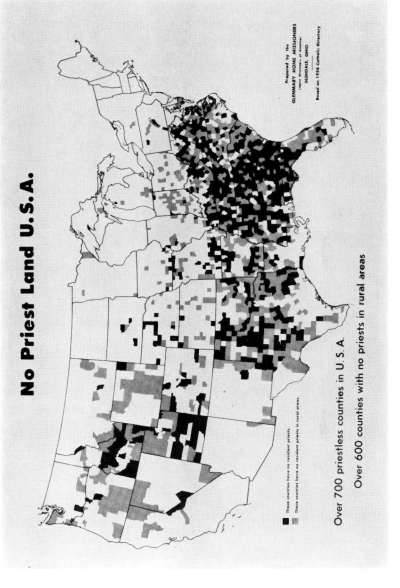

Prepared by the
GLENMARY HOME MISSIONERS
(Home Missioners of America)
GLENDALE, OHIO

Based on 1958 Catholic Directory

■ These counties have no resident priests.

▨ These counties have no resident priests in rural areas.

Over 700 priestless counties in U. S. A.

Over 600 counties with no priests in rural areas

Faculty and part of the student body, Glendale, Ohio, 1959.

CHAPTER 4

ON APRIL 16, 1917, the United States entered the World War. About the same time, Father Bishop requested Cardinal Gibbons to transfer him, preferably to a country parish where he could devote himself to rural work. At that time he knew nothing of life in a farming community. As a boy and as a man he had lived in cities, accustomed to wide contrasts of wealth and poverty. From priests of his own age he may have gathered that rural spots were unrewarding, and perhaps that impression may have influenced him to offer his services for the love of God as the pastor of a humble, obscure parish. It was not until Saturday, September 8, however, that the Cardinal informed him he had been selected to succeed Father John Liljencrants at the Church of St. Louis King, Clarksville, Maryland.

St. Louis King is the central parish of Howard County, which lies along the eastern edge of the Piedmont plateau and was originally settled in 1649, at least sparsely, by Puritans from Virginia, who were granted asylum in Maryland by its Catholic governor. In 1700 a grant of 10,000 acres in Howard County was made to Charles Carroll, on which he built Doughoregan Manor. The only known Catholics in Howard County were probably Charles Carroll and whatever Catholic retainers and slaves he held at the Manor. The first Church of St. Louis King was built in 1855 and the second, still in use, in 1889.

It is interesting to note from the 100th anniversary booklet on St. Louis Church that throughout the years it held an annual picnic to which the whole of Howard County turned out, in early years on horses and in carriages, and later in automobiles. Discontinued years before the advent of Father Bishop was a tournament at the picnic when young men of the parish with lance at rest drove their horses down a course in the meadow behind the church, striving to pick off a ring suspended from a crossbar. As in medieval times, the apple-cheeked country girls applauded their cavaliers. The winner's lady became the Queen for the Day. Old parishioners, who were often disappointed at the weather, said the date for the picnic was the first rainy Wednesday in August. From Father Bishop's diary we know that for the first three years of his pastorate, that gloomy prediction came true.

The Church of St. Louis King, where Father Bishop was pastor for twenty years, is at a Y of two main roads, about halfway between Baltimore and Washington. It is a small Gothic church, forty feet high, with a steeple rising another twenty-five feet. The front, facing the road, is of granite blocks, with an arched doorway, above which is a stained glass circular window. The building seats about two hundred people. Trees shade the roof and vines cling to the four windows along each side. A stone's throw to the right is the rectory, a modest house, boasting at least a comfortable sitting room. To the rear of the house are spacious barns, a necessity for the early pastors who had to travel the roads in horse and buggy.

St. Mary's Chapel of Doughoregan Manor is a station of St. Louis Parish, where Father Bishop said Mass every Sunday. It is a fine colonial structure attached to a manor building, which itself is almost as well known as Mt. Vernon for its early American architecture. After the revolution of 1689 Catholics of Maryland were forbidden to hold public religious services. Mass could be said in private chapels, however, and thus it was that Charles Carroll erected St. Mary's Chapel, to which he invited his Catholic neighbors and servants whenever a Catholic priest visited the area. One enters the Chapel from the great lawn. For more than two hundred years, through wide, carved doors, farmers of Howard County passed to hear Mass.

Father Bishop bought a secondhand Ford. It had to be cranked by hand and possessed all the frailties of an automobile of that period. Its tires blew out; its battery ran down; it got stuck in ruts on the muddy roads; rain penetrated its curtains. Somehow, however, it took the young priest to St. Mary's Chapel each Sunday and to the bedside of dying parishioners within a radius of twenty-five miles of his church.

In his first year Father Bishop became acquainted with the hardships of a country pastor. In the middle of winter the coal he had purchased was used up, and the church doors were locked temporarily; Mass was said in the rectory. Collections averaged six dollars a Sunday. His first Christmas collection was sixty-five dollars. Bills accumulated against the day of the annual picnic, when he would be again in funds. On Ash Wednesday with the roads knee-deep in mud from the spring rains, only three parishioners attended the services.

Yet progress was made. A heating plant was installed in the church and on December 31, 1918, we read in his diary:

"Things I aim to accomplish sooner or later:
"1. To establish a parish school. Next fall will be the most favorable time, if it can be done.

"2. To organize catechism classes in various parts of my parish and visit them periodically; and especially a weekly class in the rectory.

"3. To start a parish paper, issued monthly, to go to every family so that nobody may be without news of his church."

CHAPTER 5

"NEXT fall" was not a favorable time. In fact it was not until two years later that the words "Parochial School" appeared for the first time in Father Bishop's announcements. His inspiration, perhaps, was his friend, Father Patrick E. Conroy of Bryantown, Maryland, who built the first Catholic rural school in the Archdiocese of Baltimore. It was this same priest who urged him later to attend a meeting when the Catholic Rural Life Conference was being organized.

His parishioners responded generously to his appeal. In one month $5,000 was pledged, but that proved to be the maximum he could expect. For the next two years he added little to the fund. In those years he was in constant pain. The jacket harness he wore did little more than permit him to walk upright. In the spring of 1922 he spent two months in Florida, seeking some measure of relief. He saw a number of specialists who prescribed a new form of brace.

Returning to Clarksville, and again somewhat his old self, he recognized that a small rural parish could not finance a school from the donations of its parishioners. He sought the help of the Catholic Daughters of America and the Knights of Columbus. He conceived the idea that if an organization was formed among the Catholic masses of the city to aid rural schools the problem could be solved. It presented to him a new challenge, the forerunner of many such. On Thanksgiving

Day, through his efforts, more than two hundred women of the Catholic Daughters of America from Washington and Baltimore attended a High Mass at St. Louis Church. Father Frank Cavanaugh sang the Mass and Father John McNamara, later a bishop, preached. At a luncheon which followed, Father Bishop formed the League of St. Louis, whose purpose was to build and maintain a parochial school in Clarksville. One thousand members were obtained, each one paying annual dues.

On May 13, 1923, Father Bishop turned the first spadeful of earth, and on September 30 of the same year a church announcement read: "Our school opens tomorrow morning, October first. Today we have the pleasure of greeting the Sisters who are to conduct St. Louis School. A glad day for our little parish. Let us be grateful to God for so great a blessing."

The school started with thirty-nine children, taught by three Sisters of the Congregation of Divine Providence of Melbourne, Kentucky. On the Sunday after the school opened, Father Bishop stood in a group admiring the small building. He said to one of his lanky parishioners: "How do you like it?" "I ain't got nuthin agin it," was the man's short response. He tried again. "Wal, it seems to me, it cud a bin two feet more out of the ground."

Father Bishop was not content to have the League of St. Louis restrict itself to his own parish. His vision had broadened to take in all the rural parishes in Maryland that needed schools. He planned a similar league in the most minute detail for all the Catholics of the Archdiocese. In June of 1924, at the request of Archbishop Curley, he submitted his plan:

"1. That the League of the Little Flower be formed, applications for membership to be made on forms provided by the Chancery.

"2. That an annual collection for the country mission

churches be taken up in the fall; that it take the form of an appeal by the Archbishop for funds and for new members.

"3. That the money raised be used for needy country parishes requiring schools.

"4. That the League of the Little Flower be the authorized official medium for collecting and disbursing the funds for such needy country parishes all over the Archdiocese.

"5. That the city pastors invite country pastors to make the appeal, when the letter of the Archbishop is read.

"6. That a regular monthly pamphlet be published by the League."

We should note that here were three of the basic tools used by Father Bishop thereafter in his life's work for rural missions: First, the publicizing of the existence and problems of such missions; second, the aid of the hierarchy; and third, the mass grouping of city dwellers in behalf of the cause.

His interest in rural schools led him to the National Catholic Welfare Conference in Washington, where he found a kindred spirit in Miss Regan, then national president of the women's group. With her he discussed plans for Rural Vacation Schools to be conducted by Sisters of the Archdiocese and financed by the National Catholic Women's group. He laid the plan before Archbishop Curley, who gave him permission to start the vacation schools in a rural parish in southern Maryland in the summer of 1925. The experiment was a success.

From this time, when Father Bishop was forty years old, every bit of his energy was directed toward building strong country parishes in the United States. The Archdiocese of Baltimore was his natural starting point. Having secured the permission of the Archbishop for a Diocesan Rural Conference, he wrote to him in Athlone, Ireland, where the good Prelate was vacationing: "Pardon me, Your Excellency, for interrupting your well-earned vacation with a little shop talk, but here it is — ."

He spelled out his plans for the first diocesan Catholic rural life conference in the United States to be held October 28, 1925, in Baltimore. Naturally, His Grace, the Archbishop, would preside. Fr. Joseph Johnson, S.J., would lead a discussion of "The Rural Parish School"; Father John LaFarge, S.J., would talk on the "Rural Parish School and the Negro"; Father Harvey Quinn would speak on "The Influence of Sisters in a Rural Community"; and Fr. Edwin V. O'Hara, later Bishop O'Hara of Kansas City, who in 1927 published his work *Church and the Country Community,* would give the keynote speech.

From a diocesan rural life conference to one on a national scale was just a step. As early as 1923 Father Bishop had attended the first National Catholic Rural Life Conference in St. Louis as a registered delegate from Baltimore. With Father O'Hara, its founder, he became a member of the first Board of Directors. In 1928 he was elected its president, succeeding Father Luckey. The following year Father O'Hara was consecrated Bishop of Kansas City and had to withdraw from active participation. That left Father Bishop with the entire responsibility.

The stock market crash in 1929 had ended the lush period of the early twenties. As a consequence, financial help was difficult to find. The new President had no money in the treasury, although there was an ample supply of stationery which he put to good use. For six years he used his own meager funds to arrange conventions and to drive from city to city on Conference business. Naturally, he surrounded himself with men equally interested in agrarianism, such as Father LaFarge, Bishop Muench of North Dakota, Father Edgar Schmiedler, and others. They urged that the well-being of the entire nation rested on a healthy agrarianism.

At every opportunity Father Bishop spoke on the spiritual and economic status of the rural group. With Bishop O'Hara he worked out a plan for aid on a national level to the dioceses in the South and Southwest, where later his missionary map showed a lack of priests. In a report to his Archbishop, who had contributed generously, he pointed out that Father John O'Hara had visited personally all the dioceses in the South and Southwest; that 83 schools were aided by the Home Mission Board in 21 dioceses; that 294 teachers had been employed; that the total number of students in a four-weeks course numbered 2732 boys and 2691 girls. As Brother Raymond Philip Witte, S.M., writes in his book, *Twenty-five Years of Crusading:* "During this period Father Bishop and the National Catholic Rural Life Conference were one. Had it not been for him, the Conference would probably not be in existence."

On November 5, 1931, Father Bishop's mother died. For seventy-eight years she had served her family and her God. To her priestly son, as he sang her Requiem, this was the beginning and not the end of her life.

In 1933 at the Milwaukee meeting of the Rural Life Conference, some of the members argued that Father Bishop and his group should share their leadership with others. The following year, 1934, Father Joseph Campbell succeeded Father Bishop as President. After the election, a purse was made up and sent to him with a permanent memorial. He replied: "I do not need to tell you that nothing of the kind was looked for when I went to St. Paul. I felt completely repaid for whatever efforts I have made for the cause that is very dear to me, by the honor, repeated year after year, of serving our group in the highest office in their power to bestow."

For almost every project of the National Rural Life Conference Father Bishop made a laboratory of his own rural parish in Clarksville. His teaching Sisters learned the art of weaving to pass it on to the farm families. To parishioners who thought of moving to the city, he pointed out that farming was a way of life never to be equaled by the routine hours of labor in a city. Among the youth he founded and fostered 4-H Clubs, hoping to create organizations similar to the young Christian Workers of France and Canada. He organized a Credit Union in his own parish and met with its Committee in granting loans to its members. He urged co-operation among the farmers to enable them to buy and sell in better markets.

The postwar depression at the beginning of 1933 had deepened to the point that agrarians like Father Bishop advocated drastic steps to bring the national economy back to a sane balance. He urged a return to the land. In the quarterly magazine called *Landward,* which he wrote, edited, and published, he placed the greatest problem of the day as that of the displaced man, deprived of an opportunity to make a living, forced against his will and his self-respect to be dependent permanently on what amounted to a dole. His solution was rehabilitation on the land, so that the unemployed whom industry could not absorb would be made self-supporting on small farms. He favored resettlement of workers in the Northwest and Alaska.

These projects kept him busy. To illustrate the strenuous day-by-day life led by Father Bishop as a country pastor, educator, and humanitarian, let's take a week in May from his diary:

"*Sunday:* First Communion, nine children — May procession, blessing of fields. In evening, meeting in Town House, Washington, with Mrs. Reynolds and others. She is deeply interested in colonization for Catholics; has had experience in Oregon as an expert lobbyist.

"*Monday:* Mass at 7:30. Special 4-H Club meeting with Mr. Jenkins, Father Thompson and Jack Moore.

"*Tuesday:* Read paper on "Seal of the Confessional" at quarterly clerical conference.

"*Wednesday:* After May devotions went to Baltimore to get first issue of *Landward* off the press.

"*Thursday:* Ascension Day. Mrs. Murphy came to Clarksville in afternoon to mimeograph covering letter to go with *Landward* to Board of Directors of National Catholic Welfare Conference.

"*Friday:* First meeting of Governor's Committee of seven to administer relief funds. Children's entertainment in evening.

"*Saturday:* Went to Washington; saw Senator Bankhead about his bill for farm colonization and settlement. Said Department of Agriculture was cool and National Grange, hostile."

In the twenty-fifth anniversary report of the Harvard class of 1910 Father Bishop listed his occupation as "Catholic Priest." There was never any doubt of this. His primary purpose in life was the offering of the Divine Sacrifice for his own soul and the souls of those entrusted to him. Most of those souls were farmers; their problems were his problems. Their daily lives, in order to be successful, had to be lived in accordance with true moral principles. His tireless energy and the brilliance of his imagination led him farther and farther in efforts to better their material condition.

In 1934 his plan for the formation of a Catholic colonization project crystallized. Again, his own parish was to be the laboratory. His plan had been carefully thought out with Father Luigi Ligutti, later Executive Secretary of the National Catholic Rural Life Conference, who at that time was in the process of forming a part-time farming community in his rural parish at Granger, Iowa. Father Ligutti's negotiations in Washington for financial help under the National Industrial Recovery Act were ably assisted by Father Bishop, who in large measure was responsible for the final official approval.

In the Chancery Office at Baltimore Father Bishop filed a detailed statement of his colonization objectives for the perusal of the Archbishop. He intended to acquire three farms, totaling four hundred acres, a mile from his Church, on which forty Catholic families, moved from Baltimore, would occupy forty farms with a central house for administration and instruction and a civic library. Small co-operative enterprises, such as a cannery and a cheese factory, would add to the farm income as well as a roadside market and a consumer's co-operative store in Baltimore. Plumbers, tailors, carpenters would ply their trades; a doctor and a veterinarian would provide their professional services. The land would be purchased through state and federal grants with on obligation on the community to repay over a long period of years.

Father Bishop pursued his objectives with characteristic energy. He obtained options on the land. He drew plan after plan of small colonial houses, tree-shaded streets, and a Catholic Church, rising above the landscape. It was approved by Catholic prelates such as Bishop O'Hara, although his own Archbishop was noncommittal. His very close friend and confidante, **Father McAdams, told him frankly it was impractical. He** conferred several times with Henry Wallace, the Secretary of Agriculture, and apparently enlisted the sympathy of Harry Hopkins, Secretary of the Interior; so much so that he was promised an interview with the President of the United States, Franklin Roosevelt, which never materialized. He interested the political leaders of Maryland, who promised but did not provide help.

On Christmas Day, 1934, he asked his congregation to pray for the success of an intention dear to his heart; and on a succeeding Sunday he told his people of his plan. He soon found that his own farm folk had wills of their own. Most of them opposed the idea. Several went to the Commissioners of Howard County and protested against a new community of "city farmers" in their midst. In his diary on January 23, 1935 Father Bishop noted that his project was killed. He could not alienate any of his parishioners. He harbored no resentment, nor did his parishioners doubt the sincerity of his purpose.

Time proved them right. Today the city has moved to Clarksville; from Baltimore to Washington subdivisions stretch in an unbroken line. Across the highway from the Church a builder has set up city streets and residences. Today the school is overcrowded and not with the children of farm families, but with the children of suburbanites.

CHAPTER 6

AMONG the aims of the Catholic Rural Life Conference was the strengthening of country parishes and the creation of new ones. No advocate had stated them better than Bishop Edwin O'Hara, the founder of the Conference: "In God's own season and by God's own power to provide, ten thousand new Catholic parishes may come to decorate the landscape in our nation's remoter districts; ten thousand parishes manned by ten thousand quality priests, who recognize and respect the rural apostolate for what it is."

Inspired by these perhaps prophetic words, Father Bishop had been influential in having the Conference provide summer vacation schools for the teaching of Catholicity in the South. He had never been satisfied that these annual forays answered the need. At the termination of his colonization project, he thought more and more of the problem. Perhaps the failure of his colony plan evidenced the directing hand of God. Had the idea succeeded, his lifework would have been diverted into a completely different channel. As it was, there was no vacuum left by his defeat. Deeply embedded in his conscious mind was a plan for the grouping of mass strength toward the spreading of the Catholic Faith in the remote rural areas of America.

Father Bishop had long since abandoned the intellectual

attitude of pointing to necessary tasks and leaving the doing of them to others. He had built in himself an urge for accomplishment. Not satisfied with doing well the chores of a country parish and the maintenance of his church and school on a sound financial basis, he had actively directed the Rural Life Conference, of which he had been the president. He managed the affairs of the League of the Little Flower, editing its monthly news. He published and wrote *Landward,* the quarterly periodical of the Conference. He lectured on rural problems at the Catholic University of America and read papers at diocesan clerical meetings arranged by the Archbishop. He never missed his annual retreat in which he returned wholeheartedly to meditation, reflection, and prayer.

Among the first to whom he gave his plan for a new Society was, of course, his superior, Archbishop Curley the Primate of Baltimore, whose reaction was not favorable. He wrote to Father Bishop: "I studied carefully your plan for a new Religious Community for rural purposes. Frankly, I cannot see it in the light of our own needs here in the Archdiocese of Baltimore. If someone wants to have something like it in the middle West or the far West they might take it up, but I cannot see my way clear to give it approval or to sanction a motherhouse within the limits of this Archdiocese. We have all the religious orders that the Church needs, as far as I can see. But I am expressing my own opinion only. You are perfectly free to take it up with the Apostolic Delegate or other members of the hierarchy who may see something in it. Every good wish."

In May of 1935, Father Bishop stopped at Maryknoll on the Hudson River to see its superior, Bishop Walsh. He knew that Father Tom Price, a co-founder of Maryknoll, and a neighbor of his father in Wilmington, North Carolina, before going into missionary work in China had inaugurated the North Carolina Apostolate. Father Bishop suggested, as an alternative to the founding of a new society, that the Bishop might permit him to come to Maryknoll and start a co-ordinated branch to do missionary work in the United States. Bishop Walsh did not encourage the proposal. But he did say: "Your work must be done. It should have been started fifty years ago."

Bishop Walsh promised that if such a society could be started, separate and apart from his own Community, Maryknoll would train its first priests. He gave Father Bishop a copy of the Maryknoll Constitution and pledged his co-operation.

A year passed in which the plan gradually took form. Father Bishop lost no opportunity of talking about it to his friends in the Rural Life Conference. In February of 1936 he returned to the home of his father in Wilmington, North Carolina, where his old Aunt Lizzie was still living. Little had been done since his father's day to spread Catholicity in the priestless counties of that state. In Raleigh, North Carolina, he received a gracious reception from Bishop Hafey, who welcomed the thought of assistance from a band of missionaries in his diocese. Within the year the Bishop had revived the North Carolina Apostolate, established by Father Tom Price. With Bishop Hafey Father Bishop visited Father Irwin, a veteran missioner in New Bern, North Carolina. Their discussion lasted until the wee hours of the morning. Father Irwin offered much valuable advice. Both he and Bishop Hafey thought the proposed society should confine itself to activities in the southern states. Father Bishop thought otherwise. He visualized a society on a national scale, one that through successive generations could be properly termed "The Home Missioners of America."

On March 27, 1936, the *Ecclesiastical Review* contained as its leading article Father Bishop's plan for an American Society of Catholic Home Missions to operate in the rural sections of the United States. He proposed to form a society of secular priests, content with a modest beginning and a slow, steady growth as God would send subjects and funds. When possible to do so, Brothers and a community of Sisters would be added. The Society should have a mother house located in farming country near a large city. The mother house should be a home for the priests and Brothers while not on the missions and a novitiate and seminary for young men preparing for ordination. Sisters would train as social workers, visitors, and parish school teachers, with the domestic arts as sidelines. The priests would be instructed in a special technique of spreading the Gospel in rural sections, adapted from the methods of present home and foreign missionaries.

Having been invited to do missionary work in a given diocese, the Superior General of the Society would ask the Ordinary to assign to the Society one rural parish, miles from any neighboring parish, in a section overwhelmingly non-Catholic. Two resident priests of the Society would be the pastor and assistant. To such a parish each year would be sent two missionary priests, equipped with a tent and a portable altar and accompanied by Brothers. These missioners would adopt the camp meeting idea, so familiar in the Protestant South. During the summer, vacation schools of religion would be conducted for the children of the area.

The Society would be composed of secular priests, without vows, banded together for a common purpose. As soon as an area allotted to the Society could be sufficiently developed, it would be turned over to the diocesan clergy and the priests of the Society would move on to new frontiers. They would be the advance guard, the shock troops to open up new and hostile territory.

In deep humility, Father Bishop ended his article: "It is in no spirit of presumption that the writer presents for discussion and comment by the clergy his plan for an American Society of Catholic Home Missions, but rather with the greatest eagerness that hands abler and worthier than his own may be found to put it into execution if it be God's will that it should be carried out."

Father Bishop had never accepted Archbishop Curley's letter as a complete disapproval of his plan. Between the lines he thought he detected a real interest, if not an urge to sponsor the plan himself. But his Superior was a very busy man and, unfortunately, in such failing health that periodic visits to the hospital were necessary. In April of 1936 for the first time since January he saw the Archbishop in his room at the hospital. He looked worn and ill and admitted that he was very tired. "But not too tired," he said, "to talk of your plan."

It was evident that the Archbishop once again fell under the influence of the quiet-speaking priest, whom he had fostered for so many years, and whom he loved truly as a son. Archbishop Curley was an outspoken man, rarely a diplomat, but as Father Bishop often said, he had a heart of gold. The Prelate's permanent impression of the priest was that he was a gentle man of God, highly impractical, but somehow or other accomplishing worthy ends without any apparent ability. The Archbishop just didn't trust his own judgment when dealing with Father Bishop; and he told him again that such a Society was not for the Diocese of Baltimore. Certainly there were other bishops in the Far West or in the Middle West who could sponsor a Home Mission Society as well as he could. Let Father Bishop send his plan to as many bishops as he thought wise; and if the Apostolic Delegate were willing, why not quote the statement he had made approving the plan.

Father Bishop was delighted. Before he left he knelt to receive the Archbishop's blessing.

Among his close friends in Washington was Father McAdams, the pastor of St. Joseph's Church in the shade of the Capitol, a priest who had known Father Bishop as an assistant to Father Craig at the Shrine of the Sacred Heart in Mt. Washington. Father McAdams had eased his problems as a curate, and had helped him in enlisting the Catholic Daughters of America in the cause of a new school at Clarksville. He had told him frankly that his colony plan was impracticable. In fact he commented on it in picturesque American slang. "It's a crack-pot idea," he said.

To him Father Bishop came again for advice. Father McAdams suggested ways and means of making contacts with members of the American Hierarchy. He stressed the necessity of obtaining words of approval from many bishops, even if circumstances were such that no invitation to start in any particular diocese could be expected.

In May Father Bishop met with Father Donald Hayne of Davenport, Iowa, who taught religion at Mt. St. Mary's Seminary. Shortly after the publication of the plan, Father Hayne had visited him in Clarksville and offered himself as the first disciple. Later he wavered. He was still wrestling with the problem and Father Bishop suggested a Novena to the Holy Spirit, ending Pentecost Sunday. Father Hayne was the first of many priests whom Father Bishop invited to join him. During this entire trying period, when he sought the support of the hierarchy, the rural priest felt alone. If he could only have a fellow priest, who had the urge to give his energy to the cause! Yet, he thoroughly agreed with Father McAdams that just any priest attracted by a new idea could be detrimental rather than helpful.

On his first day of "missionary shopping" as he termed it in his diary, he drove to Harrisburg, Pennsylvania, where he talked to Bishop Leach. The interview was short, but long enough to convince him that the Bishop approved his plan. In the course of the conversation, Bishop Leach told him that he had five counties in his diocese without a resident priest.

In Trenton, New Jersey, without an appointment, he waited for three hours for Bishop Kiley, in the meantime making an advocate of Father Reilly, the Chancellor. In Newark, Bishop Walsh could not be seen, but his Chancellor, Monsignor Delaney, was not impressed. In Brooklyn, the Vice-Chancellor, Father Griffiths, could not arrange an interview with Bishop Molloy. In Hartford, Connecticut, Bishop McAuliffe, later a stanch supporter, could not be seen. And so ended his first "missionary shopping." The difficulties of his task became apparent. Selling maps in the New England States, a job he had done well in his student days at Harvard, was easy by comparison.

A happy thought came to him in June. In his presentation of the plan he lacked tangible, concise evidence of the need for rural priests. Certainly he could quote Bishop O'Hara and others, but he had nothing he could lay on the table and say, "Here in a nutshell is the situation of the Church in the rural counties of America." He started the Sisters of his school, including Sister Mary Providence, later located at Cynthiana, Kentucky, in searching the Catholic Directory to ascertain the number of counties in the United States having no resident priests and those without priests in the rural areas. He planned a map with priestless counties colored black, and those without priests in rural areas, gray. The map was not finished until years later, but today it shows graphically the tremendous black area in which the Church is completely absent from the domestic scene. It is being used continuously and year by year, now that the Society is established, over one hundred of the black areas have turned gray, and at least fifty gray areas white.

In the same month of June Bishop Hafey of North Carolina came to Clarksville, anxious to use the efforts of Father Bishop in his own diocese. It was a tempting offer. He proposed that Father Bishop start with a band of missionaries he would recruit in Pamleto County, where a start could be made in the mission field. He argued that from such a mission territory, the Society could branch out with evidence to support it. Father Bishop again approached his old friend, Father Mc-Adams, who advised him that such an undertaking would result in a local foray only.

The "missionary shopping" soon bore fruit. In Hartford, Bishop McAuliffe, a friendly, aged Bishop who reminded him of Bishop Shahan of Washington, had read his plan in the *Ecclesiastical Review* and gave it his unqualified endorsement. More than that, wholly without solicitation he gave Father Bishop a check for one thousand dollars for use in the work.

In New York Monsignor McIntyre, representing Cardinal Hayes, made it plain that the Cardinal would not endorse his plan, nor would he disapprove it; but he suggested that Father McDonnell, then head of the Propagation of the Faith, might be helpful. Father McDonnell received him graciously and discussed the plan for some time. He pointed out that many communities had been started, and that many had adopted methods of financing that were distasteful to the Cardinal. Father Bishop assured him that the Home Missioners Society, if erected, would never depart from conservative financing. Father McDonnell then said that the chances of success were slight; and that other home missioner groups were in the field, seeking the endorsement of His Eminence. To this Father

Bishop replied that he was convinced no other community was devoting all its energy to this one cause, nor intended to do the specialized work that the Home Missioners would do. Father McDonnell wished him success. His parting words were: "Father, you certainly need God's help — and I will pray for it."

In Cleveland, Bishop Schrembs gave a general endorsement to the plan, but said his See was not the place to start. He suggested a location in a more westerly city.

In Fargo, North Dakota, Bishop Muench, who had been selected as the new honorary president of the Rural Life Conference, discussed Conference affairs with him. As kindred spirits they talked of the quarterly, *Landward,* for which the Bishop was writing an article. They spoke of the difficulty of interesting the metropolitan bishops in the needs and problems of rural life.

Father Bishop gave the impression of being a quiet gentleman, one who would hesitate to discuss his problems with a stranger. Certainly no one ever characterized him as a suave talker, or as an extrovert, who was the friend of everyone he met. Yet he had become a veritable "Hound of Heaven" in seeking his objectives. In September he saw and interviewed Cardinal Dougherty of Philadelphia. Father Bishop found him as affable and as easy to talk to as his own Archbishop. During the conversation the Cardinal asked him about the attitude of Archbishop Curley. He replied frankly that he had not convinced his Superior of the need for a new Society, but he had been given permission to seek converts outside the Archdiocese. The Cardinal smiled. Later he said such a Society was needed, and he heartily endorsed the idea. Father Bishop suggested that with the Cardinal's sponsorship, the Society could be established in Philadelphia and be certain of success. The Cardinal promised to give it careful consideration.

In October, Father Bishop attended the Catholic Rural Life Conference at Fargo, North Dakota, determined to have the Convention adopt a resolution declaring that the countryside still remained the great home mission field; that there was an urgent need for a religious community of priests and lay brothers which would devote itself entirely to the rural mission field; that there was a need for a community of Sisters, dedicated to the same cause, whose work would be integrated with the religious community of men; that through the combined efforts of these two communities, a solidarity would be given to missionary efforts in the home mission field.

Father Bishop headed the Resolutions Committee. Despite the approval of Bishop O'Hara, Father LaFarge, and others, he could obtain only what he called a "mincing" resolution favoring a new community. Actually, the resolution was adopted almost verbatim in the *Manifesto* published by the Rural Life Conference in 1938. At that time, however, Father Bishop had already been sponsored by His Grace, the Archbishop of Cincinnati.

The year of 1937 began with a meeting of nine priests of the Baltimore Archdiocese to plan ways and means of furthering the Society of Home Missioners. At the suggestion of Father McAdams, it was agreed that Father Bishop should speak to seminarians in all the seminaries of the East. Someone suggested a League of Prayer, and all the priests agreed to carry the intention in their daily Masses.

In February Father Bishop completed a prayer he had written to be used by the friends of the rural missions. Composing it had been a trying task. He finally discarded his own in favor of one by Father Xavier Sutton, after adapting it to his own purpose. In his diary Father Bishop wrote: "A prayer is not a creation of the mind, but of the heart."

The problem of locating the headquarters of his Society weighed heavily on his mind. Perhaps Hartford was the place and Bishop McAuliffe, who believed in him, was the man to sponsor him. And so he requested permission to begin in Hartford. The Bishop approved, but said he would ask his Consultors and abide by their decision. They agreed unanimously that there was no room for another community in Hartford and that, in any event, Hartford had a dense Catholic population and was too far from the mission field. Although disappointed, Father Bishop knew they were right.

In March of 1937, Father McAdams called a meeting at his rectory in Washington. Among the priests present were Fathers Purcell, Schmidt, LaFarge, Byrnes, Mulloy, and the veteran missionary, Father Irwin — all from other dioceses and friends of rural missions. From his own Archdiocese were Fathers Bucky, Connell, O'Hara, Buckley, Ryan, Achstetter, Coady, Kamleiter, Wheeler, and of course, Father McAdams. The principal question discussed was presented by Father McAdams: "And where, Howard, will you get the funds to carry on?" Father McAdams, now a monsignor, chuckles when he recalls Father Bishop's answer: "Of course, from the seven corporal works of mercy!" Everyone present knew it was his way of saying that God would provide. The group considered the possibility of success with many bishops. Father McAdams suggested that Bishop Ireton of Richmond, Virginia, was the likeliest prospect. All agreed to offer their Lauds in the Divine Office each day for God's blessings on the new Society.

Father Bishop lost no time in driving to Richmond. At the Bishop's house he asked that he be permitted to start his

Community in the Diocese of Richmond. The answer came with great difficulty. Bishop Ireton readily agreed that in his diocese there were many counties without priests. Recently he had formed a mission band under Father Stevens, one of his own priests, who was enthusiastic in his plans for a rural apostolate. But would Richmond be the place to start? It was close to Baltimore, where Archbishop Curley had offered nothing but his good wishes. Bishop Ireton feared that to invite Father Bishop into his diocese would be indirectly an admission that his own band of missioners might prove incompetent.

"God knows," he said, "a community such as you propose is necessary, but to start it here is impossible."

Father Bishop pressed no further. He said: "Your Excellency, whom would you suggest I try?"

Bishop Ireton replied: "Why don't you talk to Archbishop McNicholas of Cincinnati? I will give you a letter to him."

Back in Clarksville, Father Bishop's spine threatened to incapacitate him. He had recently removed the brace, worn since his ordination. Doctor Lenhart of Baltimore prescribed daily painful exercises. In his diary, Father Bishop wrote: "Can this be a preparation for my task?" It was a positive answer to suffering. His will accepted it as a reality, which in the nature of things was to be borne impersonally as the will of God.

Just before his visit to Cincinnati, Father Bishop attended a meeting of the Catholic Rural Life Conference in St. Louis. He was on the Committee to draw up a Manifesto on Catholic Agrarianism. Finally printed in 1939, it received the imprimatur of Aloisius J. Muench, Bishop of Fargo, North Dakota. Chapter IX on Rural Church Expansion was written largely by Father Bishop.

On this western trip, Father Bishop stopped in Cincinnati, and on April 17, 1937, we find underscored in his diary: "THE ARCHBISHOP OF CINCINNATI AGREES TO HEAD-QUARTER MY SOCIETY."

CHAPTER 7

UPON his return to Clarksville from Cincinnati, Father Bishop consulted Doctor Motry, a noted canonist of the Catholic University, who made him aware that the Catholic Church is as insistent on technical safeguards in the founding of societies as the English chancellors were in the formation of private corporations. But Doctor Motry found no insuperable obstacles in the establishment of a Society of Secular Priests under Church law.

Later in the spring of 1937 Archbishop McNicholas came to Frederick, Maryland, near Washington, to preach at the Field Mass of the Catholic Students Mission Crusade. Father Bishop found that the Archbishop had not forgotten his promise. In fact, he outlined to the missionary priest plans for his start in Cincinnati. In a rural parish near the city the Archbishop would locate him temporarily while the priest gathered his forces. He made it clear, however, that substantial funds would not be at his disposal. Father Bishop should know that the financing of his project had of necessity to be solved by him. But the Archbishop was convinced that through proper publicity Father Bishop could build up a following of Catholic laymen to help him. It would take time certainly but, if God willed it, the time could be short. In any event, when Archbishop McNicholas returned to Cincinnati, he would write Archbishop Curley, receive his formal reply and, if it were favorable,

Father Bishop could sever his ties to the Baltimore Archdiocese and come to Cincinnati in July.

It must be remembered that Father Bishop was fifty-one years old and in poor health. He had been a pastor at Clarksville for twenty years. Those had been happy years. The thoughts of leaving his parish children, his church, and the pleasant Maryland countryside was a sword that pierced his heart. In his diary on May 17 we read: "Spent a good part of the day at Blick's farm with the children and Sisters who went there on an all-day picnic." Much is left unsaid, but between the lines we can picture the soft-speaking priest, sitting in the spring sun of a Maryland day, surrounded by his teaching Sisters and his own parish children, each one of whom he had baptized. And all this peaceful security he was about to abandon!

On May 29, 1937, Archbishop McNicholas wrote Archbishop Curley. Among other things he said: "I am too old to encourage new works, but as I told Father Bishop, I am afraid not to encourage his society. For five years I have been considering with the late Bishop Walsh of Maryknoll the necessity of a society of diocesan priests for home mission work. If Your Excellency thinks well to give a letter to Father Bishop I shall be pleased to let him start in this Diocese. I can appoint him as Vicarium to a rural parish which will enable him to make a simple stand without increasing any financial obligations."

To which Archbishop Curley replied: "I have given Father W. Howard Bishop a letter permitting him to leave the Archdiocese of Baltimore for the purpose of forming the community of which he is thinking. Father Bishop as a priest is an excellent one, none better; but he is not a hundred per cent when it comes to the question of executive ability. He has done splendid work in a little rural parish here and he has carried on with real zeal the work of the Little Flower. There is need to recommend him to your kindness. I know that you will be kind to him."

One could well differ with the good Archbishop in his appraisal of Father Bishop's executive ability. The handling of men is described ordinarily as the mark of a good executive. Had the Archbishop thought for a moment, he might have realized that with respect to himself Father Bishop had shown an excellent managerial ability. Certainly he had obtained the finest co-operation from His Excellency in the furtherance of the League of the Little Flower, in the starting of vacation religious schools, in the successful holding of the first diocesan rural conference in the United States. Was not a fine executive ability required in building up, as its President, the influence of the National Catholic Rural Life Conference? Did it require no executive ability to remain the beloved pastor of a rural church for twenty years? Was there any executive ability in editing and publishing *Landward* and *The Little Flower Magazine?* The good Archbishop in his terminology may well have defined "executive ability" as a dogmatic mastery in the handling of men, but who would question that the results obtained by a man through drawling peaceful logic were accomplished by equal, if not better, executive ability?

On the last Sunday in June Father Bishop introduced his successor, Father Leary, to his parishioners. He bade them farewell. Much to his surprise, the people of St. Louis Church gave him one hundred dollars, and those from Doughoregan Manor, one hundred thirty dollars. With the money he had received from Bishop McAuliffe and some other donations, his Society had two thousand dollars with which to start the new enterprise.

As yet there was but one member, Father Bishop himself.

Two priests of the Baltimore Archdiocese had sought leave to follow him, but the permission of the Archbishop could not be obtained. Some seminarians at St. Mary's were interested in home mission work, but at the moment no plans could be made for them.

On Sunday, July 11, 1937, Father Bishop said the early seven o'clock Mass at St. Joseph's Church in Washington. Father McAdams said the six o'clock Mass. At nine o'clock in Father Bishop's car they started for Cincinnati. Father McAdams, now a Monsignor, recalls that when he entered the automobile he asked his traveling companion if he had plenty of gas. "Certainly," said Father Bishop. I put some in a few days ago." Just outside Washington, the engine died. "Look at the gas tank," said Father McAdams. It was empty. Monsignor McAdams chuckles when he tells the story. "Howard," he says, "was the most impractical man I ever knew to obtain such practical results."

Through northern Virginia, western Maryland, and West Virginia they drove over narrow, winding roads to Parkersburg, where they spent the night. After Early Mass the next day they crossed the Ohio River. They were in the state where, as Father Bishop said, the Home Missioners might take root and send out their tendrils into remote rural areas.

In the afternoon they arrived at St. Martin's, Ohio, and its small church of the same name, where Father Bishop was officially appointed pastor by Archbishop McNicholas. There to meet them was Father Raphael Sourd, the Spiritual Director of St. Gregory's Seminary in Cincinnati. St. Martin's is a rural parish in the midst of reasonably good farm land. As early as 1820, several Catholic families had settled at St. Martin's thirty miles northeast of Cincinnati on the east branch of the Miami River. A landowner offered a tract of land for a Catholic

Church built in 1831 by Father Kundig, a missionary from Cincinnati. Nearly everyone within a radius of four miles was Catholic. Across the road from the church was the Convent of the Brown County Ursuline Nuns. Eight miles away was the mission church of Blanchester, where there were but few Catholics in contrast to St. Martin's. In the nearby towns of Westboro, Midland, and Lynchburg there was neither priest nor mission church.

As the months passed Father Bishop wrote letters of appeal to thousands of the laity in Baltimore; preached and took up collections in Cincinnati, Maryland, Pennsylvania, and New York. Gradually, his treasury increased, but his search for priests to aid him met with no success. As he wrote his former superior in Baltimore, he was in a very receptive frame of mind for accepting priest volunteers. True, applications had not been wanting, but he had found none whom he felt could shoulder the initial responsibility with him. "But," as he wrote, "I am willing to wait not only watchfully, but searchingly, until God shall send me the right material."

The work proceeded slowly. At times Father Bishop felt it was lagging hopelessly, but he did not despair. In a question period before a group of seminarians, one asked him: "How many members do you have?"

"Three. I, Myself, and Me," answered the priest, "and our decisions are unanimous."

To the seminarians at St. Gregory's Preparatory Seminary in Cincinnati, Father Bishop explained his missionary map and talked hopefully of a revision. The students in the first year of philosophy, under the leadership of Thomas Pater, now a priest faculty member and librarian at Mt. St. Mary's Seminary, Norwood, Ohio, and Ralph Asplan, now a monsignor and treasurer of the Archdiocese of Cincinnati, offered their help.

Two or three teams were organized to gather the statistics. They listed every county in the United States as either having resident priests or none. The resulting revised missionary map provided a much more descriptive appeal than the sketchy map, started by the Sisters at Clarksville, Maryland, and used by Father Bishop in his search for a sponsor. Thousands of these missionary maps were printed on cards, with the prayer for home missions on the reverse side, and widely distributed. They spoke eloquently in behalf of his Society, but he lacked a periodical, such as *Landward* and the *Bulletin of the Little Flower*. He knew a publication was essential for success, but a name for it eluded him. He thought of and discarded a dozen apt titles, until one day in his own personal prayers he asked for Divine Aid in the challenge he had accepted. The word *challenge* shone like a neon light, and so *The Challenge* was born.

Number One of Volume One appeared in February, 1938. The missionary map on the first page, revised with the help of the students at St. Gregory, demonstrated through its gray and black areas the need for a Society of Home Missioners. *The Challenge* consisted of four packed pages carrying a corner insert suggesting donations. Among its contributors were John T. McNicholas, Archbishop of Cincinnati; James E. Walsh, Superior General of Maryknoll; and John F. Noll, Bishop of Fort Wayne, Indiana. Among the first to respond was Archbishop Curley of Baltimore who sent his check for five hundred dollars. Father Bishop was delighted. While the Cincinnati clergy had received him with open arms, this gift bridged the miles between him and Clarksville, bringing back a rush of pleasant memories.

The year passed. The slow progress was disheartening. Everywhere Father Bishop visited, the hierarchy now approved.

Seminarians to whom he talked spoke earnestly of their desire to work in the mission field. *The Challenge* brought hundreds of letters, many of them with donations. But not a single priest joined him. Father Raphael Sourd remained his most likely prospect, but as yet had not made his decision. Father Bishop worked alone with bulldog tenacity. He wrote and published the second issue of *The Challenge* in the summer. Bishop Muench of Fargo, Bishop Rummel of New Orleans, Archbishop Gerken of Santa Fe, and Bishop Conroy of Ogdensburg were among those writing their congratulations. A corner card asked for vocations to the priesthood, to the Brotherhood, to the Sisterhood of the Society. If the Society itself had not grown, at least *The Challenge* had. It was now eight pages instead of four.

In July, a year to the day since he and Father McAdams entered the rectory of St. Martin's to be greeted by Father Sourd, Earl McGrath, a second year philosophy student at St. Gregory's Seminary, came to Father Bishop to tell him he had decided to join. He had the approval of Father Roddy, his rector. The Society then numbered its founder and one postulant.

Later the same month Father Bishop made an eight-day retreat at the Trappist Monastery in Gethsemane, Kentucky. To him it was an agrarian paradise with its branches in heaven and its roots in the soil. Through narrow windows he saw the brown-clad monks moving in the hot sun between carefully planted rows of corn and beans. Silence hung like a precious veil on the rooms and corridors, shielding them from the noises of the world. Early in the morning before the sun came up, the chant of Matins and Lauds whispered in the high chapel. As Father Bishop said, "Here the spirit assumes its proper proportion." He drank a long deep draught of the spiritual life. It invigorated him, brought renewed hopes for the future and a strong conviction that the cause he pressed was God's will.

In St. Martin the work went on, interrupted by attendance at a preconvention meeting of the Board of Directors of the Catholic Rural Life Conference at Vincennes, Indiana. Two secretaries were kept busy at the new office in the Fenwick Boys' Club on East Fifth Street in Cincinnati. A trip through the mission area of Kentucky, Tennessee, and Alabama was put off month by month, until in October Father Bishop became ill and spent five days in St. Mary's Hospital. On the day he was dismissed, against the advice of the nursing Sisters he drove his own car in cloudy weather through intermittent rains to Louisville, Kentucky, and thence through priestless counties to Birmingham, Alabama. Everywhere he found a pressing need for priests. As he wrote in his diary, "One thing is certain; the field was never more ready for us than now."

Some of the pictures he took appeared in the Christmas issue of *The Challenge* of 1938, which like the second publication consisted of eight pages. It, too, bore a corner insert asking for workers in the mission field of America. As Father Bishop quoted: "The harvest is great and the laborers few."

In December, Edward Smith, a Maryknoll student, announced to Father Bishop his intention of joining the Society. So, at the end of 1938, the Society consisted of its founder and two students, Earl McGrath and Edward Smith. Its worldly wealth was slight. In a year and a half its hopes and aspirations had been so publicized that the clergy and the hierarchy were intimately acquainted with its progress. Beyond that, the mill of God was grinding slowly and none could predict that it would grind exceedingly small.

In 1939 came the death of Pope Pius XI and the succession of Pius XII.

Amid his other work, Father Bishop undertook to lecture on six successive evenings in the nearby towns of Lynchburg, Blanchester, and Batavia. Marking again a departure from ordinary rules, Father Bishop gave two of the courses in small theaters in the business sections of the towns, and one in Holy Trinity Church in Batavia, where no public hall was available. In the theaters, a group of young men and women from St. Martin's formed a choir to sing hymns.

In the summer Father Raphael Sourd, Spiritual Director of St. Gregory's Seminary, joined him. Father Bishop's prayer at last had been answered! Preceding Father Sourd were three theology students from the Cincinnati Archdiocese, Clement Borchers, Francis Massarella, and Benedict Wolf. Alphonsus Atkinson, who later became a fighter pilot in World War II, and Paul Thompson, also joined as seminarians. The first of these, Father Clement Borchers, would succeed Father Bishop as Superior General of the Society.

Prior to joining, Father Sourd tested himself by going with Father Bishop in an open-air campaign in Adams County, Ohio, a priestless region of the Cincinnati Archdiocese. They were equipped with a portable altar, a loud-speaker, a projector, slides, and screen for outdoor pictures. With St. Mary's Church at Manchester as a base, each night they preached in neighboring villages and towns.

Father Sourd recalls how he and Father Bishop, like two adventurers, drove in their sound wagon to the courthouse square of West Union in Adams County on a market day. Farmers and their children stood on the curbing of the lawn around the courthouse while others gathered in groups along the sidewalk. The sound wagon was parked at an angle to the curb; the screen was set up; the loud-speaker attached and the phonograph, with its hymn records, was prepared for use. Just as they were ready to begin, a spry little old man with a soft hat above his white hair announced through a megaphone a free show would start at once. A crowd gathered while he mounted a truck, performed some tricks of legerdemain, and then drove blindfolded around the square.

When he finished, Father Sourd turned on the church-bell record, and Father Bishop, a medicine man for God, spoke through the loud-speaker: "Your entertainer has done a remarkable thing in driving his car blindfolded. Most of us have all we can do to drive with our eyes open. But which one can say he has steered his course through life without getting into trouble with his God and his conscience? Nobody. Then why don't we turn to the Church of Jesus Christ, which He taught was His Church on earth to steer us the right way?"

The two priests held the crowd for an hour. That evening they went to another town. It was a time of high adventure for Father Bishop. Into this project he put the same intelligent approach and the same enthusiasm he used in his organizational efforts. He had a happy facility for talking to every man on his own level. Throughout his life no one ever accused him of speaking down to them.

St. Mary's of Manchester, first used as a base, became the first mission church entrusted to the Home Missioners. Adams County was a picturesque infertile land without resident priests and less than a hundred miles from Cincinnati. For more than thirty years St. Mary's Church, once attended as a mission from Ripley in Brown County, had been unoccupied, a warped and weather-beaten frame structure, waiting in cob-webbed seclusion for a more fortunate day. In the sacristy Father Bishop found a calendar of the year 1909, which marked the last year that Manchester had a regular Sunday schedule of Masses. Father Koenig, a friend of Father Sourd, took up residence there with the mission priests for three weeks, bringing his carpentry tools. When he left, the wooden church was enriched with a liturgical altar, a confessional just inside the front door, and a vestment case in the sacristy.

To St. Mary's came the first band of seminarians. True to his agrarian principles, Father Bishop taught his young men that the work of their hands was as pleasing to God as the use of their intelligence. Meditation in that tiny Church under the sanctuary lamp, proclaiming that God now resided there, strengthened their hopes that some day each would start another tiny church and hang just such a sanctuary lamp.

At the end of 1939 the Society numbered two priests and ten students at St. Mary's and St. Gregory's Seminaries in Cincinnati, the latest of whom was Francis J. Wuest, who would be ordained in 1942.

Since his arrival in Cincinnati, Father Bishop had been true to his promise to Father McDonnell, the head of the Propagation of the Faith in New York, that he would never depart from conservative methods of financing his Society. True, he had to be a beggar, but he offered in return only the satisfaction of giving to a worthy cause. He often thought of the words of Monsignor McAdams that, if the hierarchy and the clergy believed in his work, he would find them his greatest helpers. In the early years of the Society *The Challenge* was sent largely to the bishops and Catholic clergy. Their response bespoke their charity and zeal for souls. The money they sent was from their own meager purses. If their parishioners contributed, they did so because they were moved by the personal appeals of Father Bishop or Father Sourd in the churches. In Chicago, for instance, Father Bishop talked to Archbishop Stritch, later a Cardinal, who died in Rome as the Prefect of the Sacred Congregation of the Propagation of the Faith. Father Bishop's diary records the conversation:

Father Bishop: "It's nice of you to see me, Your Excellency!" He smiled. "How are you and your missionary work getting along?" Father Bishop: "The time has come, Your Excellency, when we must have champions in many places other than only in Cincinnati. I'm hoping you will be one of them."

"That ought to be easy. Your aim is to supply a great need, your plan is sound and well worked out. Vocations will come. As for my Diocese, you can appeal for vocations at Mundelein, and if any of my men want to go with you they may. Talk to the Chancellor about parishes in Chicago where you may make an appeal."

In May of 1940 the Society's office was moved from the Fenwick Boys' Club in Cincinnati's business district to larger quarters on Madison Road in the suburbs. The students visited there frequently for special talks by the two priests on missionary techniques. In July the three subdeacons, Reverend Messrs. Borchers, Massarella, and Wolf, joined them in their summer campaign in Adams County.

In November a mother house was acquired on Princeton Pike near Glendale, Ohio. The pattern set by Father Bishop in his article in the *Ecclesiastical Review* was being carried out. With funds he had carefully saved, Father Bishop bought a farm of eighty-seven acres on which stood a frame house of thirteen rooms. The depression of the thirties had not yet run its full course so that the price paid required only a small amount of borrowed money. The land was extensive enough for a few simple farm projects. The new home was not pretentious but it was well situated only fourteen miles north of downtown Cincinnati. It housed Father Bishop, Father Sourd, and the three deacons who attended classes daily at Mt. St. Mary's Seminary, nine miles away. The one long room across the middle of the farmhouse was converted into a chapel. On All Saints' Day, 1940, Father Bishop sang a High Mass with one of the deacons at the organ. High resolutions were made that day in all humility, resolutions of work and more work and prayer, with success left to the will of God.

Father Bishop was home again. No longer was he the rural pastor of St. Martin's Church. In this farmhouse he was the Father of a Community. This chapel was a House of Prayer in which his daily meditations seemed closer to the God who had befriended him. For weeks, he said, he could think of nothing but prayers of thanksgiving.

Like all American Catholics Father Bishop had a special devotion to the Blessed Virgin. He had adopted the name "Home Missioners of America" and had formed an Ohio corporation to take the legal title to the farm. But the name carried no warmth to the soul of a missionary. It was utilitarian and practical; it impressed the Catholic layman and priest with the hard cold fact of necessity, much in the same way as a sermon on the Last Judgment is necessary to a well-planned retreat; but it lacked spiritual content. Archbishop McNicholas had similar ideas. When he approved the site for the mother house, he suggested it be called "Glenmary." Father Bishop brought the name to the Community. A new spirit of love was infused into the Society. Among themselves and their friends they are "Glenmary Missioners."

Three years before, the Society had been only a name with

one member and no home. By Christmas of 1940 a great Archbishop sponsored and guided it, two priests worked incessantly to expand it, and a growing band of enthusiastic seminarians studied in preparation for the mission field that awaited them. In measuring his accomplishments, Father Bishop wrote: "The theme of our rejoicing is a fair start with an open field ahead. The work that must be done will be difficult and slow. Results, as the world is accustomed to appraise them, may seem meagre. But struggle is the characteristic of all beginnings that are worth while. We need vocations from every section of the United States. We beg our friends to continue their prayers and their giving now that we begin to see a clear path ahead."

Contributions at that time presented no problem, but vocations were another matter. Bishops for the most part permitted the missioners to talk and take up collections in parish churches, but were reluctant to allow them to seek volunteers in their seminaries. As a former diocesan priest Father Bishop understood their reluctance. He knew that each bishop found it difficult to man his own diocese. As a consequence he did not seek out seminarians, but permitted them to come to him. He stressed that obedience to their bishops was pleasing to God and he could accept them only if their bishops were willing to release them. It can be said, however, that if their bishops were satisfied that the applicants had a real vocation to mission work, they were rarely refused consent.

In June of 1941 three new priests were ordained, Father Borchers, Father Massarella, and Father Wolf. They were the first to serve under the banner of the Home Missioners. As Father Bishop wrote, "Those were days in which heart-breaking sacrifices were being demanded of men, women and children at the bayonet's point all over Europe." In our own country these men would enter a combat whose decisions would last for eternity, a combat in which the conquered would join with the conqueror in the Mystical Body of Christ.

Two other outstanding events marked the year 1941. From June to December a two-story asbestos-shingled structure, aptly called "The Barracks," was in process of erection on the Glendale farm. The farmhouse was no longer adequate for five priests, one Brother, and several deacons. Father Bishop, however, was much more interested in the second event. The Peter Kuntz family of Dayton, Ohio, donated a trailer chapel and tow car. In the trailer was an altar, a confessional, Stations of the Cross, pamphlet rack, and missionary living quarters. Anywhere, at any time, the chapel on four wheels could roll up to a busy corner in No-Priest-Town and the Holy Sacrifice of the Mass could be offered, followed by a talk by Father Bishop, Father Sourd, or one of the three young missioners. Despite his fifty-six years Father Bishop remained a crusader. In his diary he regretted the daily grind of office work that prevented him from standing in the "trenches" on the platform of the chapel car.

CHAPTER 8

WITH three priests busy in Adams County, Father Bishop sought other hidden villages nestling in the triangles of intersecting gravel roads, which might be potential centers of Catholicity in a land of no priests. To these villages came farmers who tilled submarginal land or miners who brought to the surface the muscles and sinews of our technical civilization. Some of those villages had Catholic churches, rarely used; others had none.

Bishop Cotton of Owensboro, Kentucky, suggested to him that there were many such hidden villages in his diocese. One of them was Sunfish, in Edmondson County. As a mission post, the Church of St. John the Evangelist had been attended from Leitchfield, eighteen miles away, but until recently the visits were at such long intervals as two or three times a year. Near the church a school had just been constructed by a pious parishioner. The Sisters of St. Francis taught the seventy to eighty pupils; yet there was no resident priest because none was available. This was a situation which illustrated the necessity of a mission society.

Father Bishop leaped at the chance. With Father Clement Borchers, who had been assigned to Edmondson County, he lived a week in Sunfish in what he wrote was a spacious rectory. Actually it had a kitchen and one bedroom. The water had to be brought in buckets from a cistern three hundred feet from the house, and Father Borchers cooked their meals on a coal stove. As the days went by, the young priest wondered if the Superior had moved in permanently. The fact was that Father Bishop could not tear himself away. In the morning he said Mass, and after a light breakfast walked down the gravel road, smiling at the children and farmers who passed by, breathing in the aroma of the countryside. Not since Clarksville had he felt such closeness to the tilled land and its workers.

At Glenmary his desk awaited him, piled high with correspondence. The summer number of *The Challenge* demanded attention. The blessing of the mother house by Archbishop McNicholas had to be arranged. The war with its stir and bustle of great preparations brought uncertainty to many seminarians who contemplated Glenmary. One left to become a fighter pilot.

Father Borchers was doing such splendid work at Sunfish that Bishop Cotton urged Father Bishop to take a new assignment at Russellville in Logan County, Kentucky. Again the Superior accompanied one of his young priests, Father Benedict Wolf, to that village. It was in a farming community sixty-five miles from Sunfish. On a quiet street the frame Church of the Sacred Heart stood unobtrusively, and next to it a one-story frame house. Here Father Bishop stayed for a week. He drove over the roads, muddied by the autumn rains, studying Logan and Simpson Counties which made up the mission area. He said Mass on Sunday in Franklin, twenty miles to the east of Russellville, in a dwelling one room of which was used as a chapel. Fifteen Catholics attended.

Affairs at the mother house were even more pressing than in the spring. A Dominican Sister had come to take charge of the nucleus of the Sisters' organization, which now numbered five. A new priest, Father Francis Wuest, ordained in May, had to be educated in the technique of the rural missions. The wooden chapel of St. Ann-by-the-Wayside, Adams County, had been built and the Superior had to participate in its dedication. This was another landmark. In all humility Father Bishop said Mass at the white altar and, as he wrote, offered up the pride in his heart as a tribute to God.

The year 1943 might well be termed a year of "vocation shopping." Father Bishop and Father Sourd talked to seminarians whenever they could get the consent of the bishops. Father Bishop's diary at the time resembled a railroad time table. Again he was a traveling priest with a brief case. The trains were crowded with soldiers. To get a berth was almost impossible. Fortunately, the monasteries and churches, as in the middle ages, furnished a hospice to the traveling priest. In the seminaries he found many potential missionaries for Glenmary. Before they could be accepted, however, their bishop had to release them. Father Bishop was advised by canonists that ordinaries should encourage the vocations of their seminarians to missionary societies and release them if convinced of their sincerity and if the needs of their own dioceses did not absolutely require them for that purpose. At times the zeal of the missioner led to an almost arrogant demand for what he described as "his rights." He consulted his canonist friends at the Catholic University and as good "lawyers" they advised him his "rights" were not absolute; that the success of his cause depended on the good will of the bishops. It must be said that he rarely encountered a bishop who, in the final analysis, was not governed by his conscience. Yet, after one such consultation with a canonist, we read in Father Bishop's diary a wry protest:

> "Here lies the body of Cyrus McDay,
> Who died, maintaining his right of way."

In 1943, Glenmary published four issues of *The Challenge* — spring, summer, autumn, and winter. In Ohio, one half of Scioto County, adjoining Adams County, had been added to the mission field. The new mission base was Otway, a village of two hundred people, with a lovely brick church, having a bell tower and an arched, stained glass window facing the road. Sundays found Father Bishop preaching at one or the other of the mission churches with rarely more than twenty to forty people in his audience. His sermons were prepared in advance, the wording strong and well chosen. At the mother house, when he was not traveling with a brief case, he conducted a class on "Methods to Be Used in Writing Sermons." From his notes we find he stressed the importance of word images and the necessity of using one-syllabled Anglo-Saxon words in preference to words of many syllables. He taught that good sermons should point out the beauty of religion and its positive side. "In the missions," he said, "don't tell what Protestants have failed to do, but what we Catholics do, and what our Church teaches. Tell them that the smartest thing they can do at any given time and throughout their lives is to comply with the will of God."

In the spring three Glenmary priests were ordained, Father Edward Smith, Father Earl McGrath, and Father Herman Foken. For *The Challenge* Father Bishop wrote a splendid article on their capabilities. In dealing with his young companions he exercised a matured judgment. He expected of them imagination and tremendous energy and he praised them when they measured up. But he was a hard taskmaster in insistence upon implicit obedience, although he never required from them more than he demanded of himself. It has been said he relied too much on his own activities; that he was reluctant to trust a task to his young men when he could do it himself. That seems to be a common fault in men who blaze a new trail. Who can say that the trail would have been made easier through a diffusion of leadership?

Included in the Society at this time were seven young priests, as well as Father Bishop, Father Sourd, Brother Vincent, and Brother Charles. The deep spirituality of these Brothers was a lesson in humility to the Community. Both were country boys, physically strong, filled with knowledge of the earth and its creatures. Their handiwork with saw and hammer produced strong benches and cabinets. With the help of one of these Brothers, a young missioner knew a shack could easily become a home, and a garden could take shape where otherwise a tangle of weeds would ramble in confusion. Father Bishop had known Brother Charles as a bachelor farmer in the Ohio mission area. He had found in him a religious mysticism and a consent to God's will that at times caused him to question his own impetuous rush for results.

Father Bishop soon added another project to his other activities. Near Portsmouth, Ohio, he started a "Rural Information Center," applying a city idea in a country place. While driving from Otway in Scioto County, he saw at a turn in the road a soft drink store with a huge sign which could be seen a half mile away advertising a well-known soft drink. He visualized the effect if the sign had advertised a church activity. Soon the store had a new tenant — the Glenmary Home Missioners. A painter substituted a cross for the soft drink bottle. Beneath it was the inscription "LIGHT OF THE WORLD — MY WAY OF THE CROSS." Over the door a smaller sign read: "Information About the Catholic Faith." Carl Conrad, the head of a Chicago advertising firm, who loved to turn the art of show-card and window display to the service of the Church, prepared large display signs, beautifully designed and lettered in brilliant colors. Some of them were in the window; others adorned the walls of the reception room.

Father Bishop, Father Wuest, and Brother Charles divided the interior of the store by a drapery hanging from a wire stretched from wall to wall. Brother Charles painted and decorated. A small chapel developed and another mission church served the Catholics in the neighborhood. Now there is a flourishing parish which was recently turned over by the Home Missioners to the sole control of the bishop of the Columbus Diocese.

In May of 1944 Father Bishop journeyed to Mundelein Seminary in Chicago where his first recruit from that diocese was ordained, Father John Marquardt.

On Tuesday, June 6, 1944, American troops stormed ashore on the Normandy beaches. On the same day Father Bishop spoke to his Women's Missionary Group, numbering six young women, anxious to test themselves in their first invasion of the mission field. He chose three seniors, who were also the best equipped in nursing and social work, to inaugurate the first religious vacation schools at Russellville, Kentucky. In July he left the mother-house with his charges. After a two-hundred-mile trip, they arrived in a temperature of 102. Father Bishop stood on the rectory lawn the next day as the catechists arranged a group of thirty-three children, ages three to eighteen, the small ones in the front row. The classes began. The Sisters were much less confused than Father Bishop. Their plan of teaching the Mass and the Liturgy came tumbling about their ears. What the children needed were fundamentals. After three hours of patient drill, their young charges could make the Sign of the Cross and recite the "Hail Mary" and the "Our Father." In the afternoon Father Bishop accompanied them to Johnstown, twenty-seven miles away, where ten children were seated on boxes under shade trees to learn for the first time how to make the Sign of the Cross. Father Bishop wrote in his diary: "This is a banner day for our women's group."

In September Bishop Gerald O'Hara of the Savannah-Atlanta Diocese wrote Archbishop McNicholas, urgently inviting the Home Missioners to take over a mission area of seven counties in Georgia with Statesboro as the mission center. Father Bishop's first reaction was that it was impossible. However, the Archbishop promised to help in the Ohio mission territory with a diocesan priest, and the Glenmary Missioner acquiesced. He accepted in a letter to Bishop O'Hara, though as he wrote "it strains our facilities to the cracking point."

As a good general he rearranged his troops, and on a fine Indian summer day in October drove with Father McGrath, Father Smith, and Brother Vincent to the mission field, miles away from the mother-house. After two rainy days, just as the sun began to shine they arrived at Statesboro late in the afternoon. One of the few Catholics was there to show them the bungalow topped by a large sign: "Catholic Mission Center." A painter engaged by Bishop O'Hara was finishing the exterior. It was an attractive house, built almost in the form of a cross, with the front porch hidden by shrubbery and shade trees forming a backdrop in the rear.

The only Catholic Church in the whole area of seven counties was St. Joseph's Chapel at Bay Branch, where in the first days of the mission enterprise Mass was said by Father McGrath. At the bungalow in Statesboro Father Bishop said Mass, served by Brother Vincent.

In the meantime, Father Sourd was carrying on at the home base. Certainly nothing more providential had occurred in Father Bishop's new life than the wholehearted devotion of Father Raphael Sourd in sharing his ideals. No man can live entirely alone. The two priests became close companions. Father Sourd, too, was a traveling priest with a brief case. Many, if not most, of the new members of the Society came as a result of his efforts. In emergencies, when a younger priest became incapacitated, Father Sourd as well as Father Bishop substituted in the mission churches. Together they discussed vocation problems and methods of financing. Although a younger man, Father Sourd's temperament was even and calm, much more so than that of his Superior. Each had a broadening effect on the other.

In 1945 four more priests were added to the roll: Fathers Joseph Dean and Boland from Chicago, Father Burke of the Trenton, New Jersey, Diocese, and Father Raymond Dehen from the Archdiocese of St. Paul. Twelve priests, twenty-one students, three Brothers, nine Sisters, and four Sister-aspirants now constituted the Society. Father Bishop was fifty-nine years old. His general health had improved, although St. Mary's Hospital and the Good Samaritan Hospital in Cincinnati knew him as an intermittent patient. Financially, he had succeeded in maintaining his mother house and his mission areas and in saving a small sum to start a seminary. He said himself he had no idea from what sources the money came. Suffice it to say he frowned on any plan for raising funds that he considered undignified.

In the Christmas *Challenge* of 1945, he wrote one of the most informative of his Christmas letters.

"Dear kind Friends: Once more at Christmas time God has called our young missioners to a new mission field. Last year it was Georgia that knocked at our door. This year it is Virginia, six of whose mountainous western counties will have received a mission band of two Home Missioners by the time this letter reaches you. They will live in Norton in the tiny rectory that has been built onto the rear of the Catholic Church, almost submerged even in so small a town. Appalachia, another mountain town eleven miles away, will be their mission. In these six counties covering 2700 square miles and containing 171,486 people there is only a thinly scattered population of Catholics.

"Here is a mission area that furnishes every type of problem that could face a Home Missioner; town and country, farmlands and wooded mountainsides, a mixture of foreign groups in the mining settlements; and on the slanted clearings the rugged mountain families who resent all 'furriners.' Scores of towns and villages, hundreds of miles of steep winding roadways lend flavor to the mission picture and challenge the missioners.

"And our young missioners — God bless them — are thrilled at the prospect of spending Christmas of 1945 in these surroundings among people they have never seen.

"This bit of news, dear friends, is our Christmas Greeting to you. How grateful all of us are for your help in the past! How we look forward to the building of our new seminary at Glenmary, so that our theological students at least may grow up in our midst. We beg a continuance of your valued friendship or — in case we are just getting acquainted — that our friendship may begin at once and that it may be long and mutually helpful.

"Wishing you a wealth of Christmas blessings, we are,

> Sincerely yours in Christ,
> THE HOME MISSIONERS OF AMERICA
> FATHER W. HOWARD BISHOP
> *Superior*."

Previously Father Bishop had visited Bishop Swint of the Diocese of Wheeling, West Virginia, who gave him a general outline of the Norton mission area and his problem of keeping even a visiting priest in the area on infrequent occasions. With Father Krauss, who had been serving the missions, Father Bishop drove from Norton over a little-traveled road, all mountainous and curvy, to dozens of towns and villages in the six counties entrusted to his Society. He found St. Anthony's Church in Norton, a frame structure heated by a coal stove. In Appalachia, just across the railroad tracks, stood the Sacred Heart Mission, a quaint wooden church surmounted by a tower at one of its corners. As he drove from deep valleys to high ridges, seeing below him swift streams flowing over sharp bare stones; as he saw mile after mile of scarred mountain sides and open coal pits, he knew that this was a real challenge.

In the early summer of 1946 Father Bishop made the first of his annual inspection trips to the mission fields. After two nights and twenty hours of driving, he rolled up to the white mission church at Bay Branch, Georgia. A Sunday morning sunlight beamed down on the fresh white paint of the church. From the windows came the singing voices of the Glenmary Sisters, who just a week before had opened a summer catechism school for parish children. After Mass Father McGrath introduced his Superior to the small congregation. The drawl of Father Bishop matched the "Cracker" accent of his southern neighbors. One of the parishioners had prepared a breakfast of home-cured Georgia ham and biscuits. Later they listened to the Sunday morning Catholic Hour broadcast from Savannah where Father Burke, the assistant Home Missioner in the area, was completing the fourth of his series of Sunday morning talks.

No visit to Bay Branch would have been complete without calling on Miss Molly Lehr, seventy years of age, whom Father

Bishop and the young missioners called "The Apostle of Bay Branch." For years "Aunt Mollie" had kept the Faith alive among the few Catholics around Bay Branch. In times past when a priest, at rare intervals, came from Savannah he would write her and she would see to it that all Catholics in the vicinity got to church. Under her direction the mission church was cared for, cleaned, painted, and kept ready for the infrequent services. Visiting missioners could always count on Miss Mollie's home for food and lodging. When the Glenmarians arrived Aunt Mollie adopted them. Well they remembered that first dinner at her home, crisp, brown, Georgia chicken and hickory-smoked ham. After weeks of cooking their own meals at Statesboro, they rationalized that a mission visit to Aunt Mollie was a material, if not a spiritual, necessity. Of her, Father Bishop wrote: "May God reward Miss Mollie Lehr, a home missioner *par excellence.*"

In Statesboro many Catholics had returned to the Church and the congregation had outgrown the house chapel in the six-room bungalow. Father Bishop noted that somehow his Society had to build a new church for the growing parish.

North through Georgia and the Carolinas he traveled along the ridges of the Great Smokies into Virginia and then along the Trail of the Lonesome Pine to Norton, Virginia. He was met there by three of his "boys," Father Smith, Father Dean, and Brother Anthony. With one or the other of them he visited mining camps, where lived hundreds of soft-coal miners, many of them of Catholic Slavic descent.

At Appalachia he found the Sacred Heart Church clean and redecorated. At best it had a drab exterior and within no priests could compete with the puffing locomotives that pulled gondolas filled with coal within fifty feet of the altar. A recent strike had freed a group of coal miners, who with paint, hammer, and saw, remodeled the annex of the church into two neat meeting rooms for Catholic discussion clubs. On the Feast of the Sacred Heart Father Bishop with his young missioners baptized twenty persons, young, middle-aged, and old. As he wrote, the ceremony was beautiful, thrilling, and unforgettable for anyone with the heart of a missionary.

From Norton he traveled to Otway, the first mission base in Adams County. He visited the wooden churches in Buena Vista, West Portsmouth, and Pond Creek, where nearby three Glenmary Sisters lived in a woodland camp, conducting a summer catechism school for the third year. Later in the year he visited Sunfish and Russellville in the Kentucky mission fields, and again he spoke with Father Sourd from the trailer-chapel.

At Glenmary, 1946 was a very busy and difficult year. The Society now numbered eighteen priests and, with the Brothers and Sisters, totaled more than fifty. A manual of prayers, adapted to the needs of the Community, had to be compiled. As Father Bishop had once noted in his diary, a prayer must come from the heart and not the mind. Up to this time the Maryknoll Community Prayers had been used with adaptations. Now with the aid of Father Heiring, a new recruit, he studied the prayer books of four societies and inserted the ideals and hopes of a rural missionary. When completed, it was approved by Archbishop McNicholas.

At the same time a Constitution had to be written. The Maryknoll Constitution, given to him by Bishop Walsh years ago, was examined but found vastly oversize for a small community. After a month's study, he turned to Archbishop McNicholas, who advised him that at least for the present the Constitution should provide a simple form of government without a Council and a General Chapter. The Archbishop ruled

that so much remained to be done in the formation of a Novitiate, in the building of a Superior House of Studies, and in
obtaining the approval of the Congregation of Religious in
Rome, that for the time being the Constitution might well
state only the rules governing admissions and community life
and name the persons of the governing group, including Father
Bishop as Superior. Under the direction of the Archbishop,
Father Bishop wrote a Constitution which was permitted to
be put into effect as the tentative rule of the Society.

In the building of the Home Missioners the Archbishop was
an active artisan. He counseled with its founder, at times agree-
ing with him on a worthy candidate, at other times disapprov-
ing. In the formation of the Sisters' group he was particularly
helpful. It was he who procured the Dominican Sister Kevin
and Sister Immaculata of Adrian, Michigan, to train the
women's group, numbering seventeen in 1946, in their farmhouse convent and in a small house on Oak Street in Cincinnati. The quiet spirituality of the Dominican Sisters produced
a community of self-disciplined young women, able and willing
to be exemplars of Christian charity, through which they were
to win the love of children in their "Bible classes," and the
confidence of the helpless poor in their homes.

From day to day Father Bishop planned the future. His
"boys," as he called them, now numbered twenty-three priests,
deacons, and Brothers. His Community of Sisters was taking
shape. Plans had been drawn for a seminary. He would need
teachers. With the help of Archbishop McNicholas he sent
Father McGrath and a new recruit, Father French, to study
at the Angelicum in Rome, while residing in the Casa San
Giovanni in Vatican territory.

Nor were the missions neglected. Funds for the building of
five chapels had been donated by Catholic laymen. St. Ann-by-

the-Wayside at Buena Vista had been built. A church at West Portsmouth was being erected, and churches at Statesboro, Georgia, and at Franklin, Kentucky, were in the planning stage. In the Virginia mission field parishioners at Dungannon, high in the wooded mountains, planned a log cabin church. At St. Paul, Virginia, a chapel had to be built to serve a growing parish.

Theodore Maynard in his *Story of American Catholicism* had characterized the Home Missioners of America as a "cloud no larger than a man's hand." Not much larger now, the "cloud" covered at least a few of the ten thousand parishes to be manned by ten thousand quality priests that Bishop Edwin O'Hara, the founder of the Catholic Rural Life Conference, had prayed would happen someday.

CHAPTER 9

BEFORE publishing his plan for an American Home Mission Society in 1936, Father Bishop had consulted books on Canon Law recommended by his friends at the Catholic University in Washington. Like other students, in his seminary days he had learned the rudiments of the Church Law. He knew that a religious society could be established of secular priests without vows, banded together under a Superior and a Rule in the manner of the Maryknoll Society. He was to learn that a little knowledge is a dangerous thing. Step by step, as he obtained a sponsor, as he branched out into mission fields in other dioceses, he realized that his Society had to become a moral entity in the eyes of the Church in order to assure it a permanent existence, aside from the good will of Archbishop McNicholas and his successors. He was certain his Society was fully established on February 25, 1944, when the Archbishop by letter erected the Home Missioners as a diocesan society, retroactive to August 15, 1939.

In 1944 and in 1945 His Grace had corresponded with the Sacred Congregation of Religious in Rome. Questionnaires had been mailed back. In 1946 Father Bishop prepared a tentative Constitution and formulated a Prayer Manual. He wrote a brief topical history of his Society. Canonists were consulted, and a volume of papers, many of them technically written in Latin, were sent to Rome by the Archbishop, together with a request for a "Decree of praise," which, if granted, would be followed by pontifical approval. With the consummation of that step, the Home Missioners of America would be free of diocesan supervision. The Archbishop and Father Bishop both awaited an answer from Rome.

None came, and in the spring of 1947 Archbishop McNicholas suggested a visit to Rome to expedite action. Father Bishop prepared himself. He had sold his plan to numerous bishops and now he had the task of persuading the officials of the Congregation of Religious that his Society was a permanent organization of the Church, worthy of papal approval.

From Bishop O'Hara, from Bishop Muench, from Bishop Ireton, and others he received letters, praising his work and suggesting the continuing need for his missionary activities in the rural areas of America. From the Apostolic Delegate in Washington he obtained a letter of introduction to Archbishop Posetti of the Congregation of Religious and to Monsignor Montini, the acting Papal Secretary of State. With Father Bishop would go a personal message from Archbishop McNicholas to his fellow Dominican, Father Skeehan, Procurator General of the Dominicans.

On May 28, 1947, Father Bishop and Father Sourd flew from Newark airport to Gander in Newfoundland and then over the sea in the dark of night to the Azores, where a brilliant sunrise greeted them. Over Portugal and Spain they looked down on treeless mountains until the blue Mediterranean and the coast of Italy spread beneath them. At Ciampino Airport in Rome their plane taxied to a stop.

On Saturday, the eve of Trinity Sunday, both said Mass in the Basilica of St. Peter. Almost lost in the great sacristy, Father Bishop vested and walked miles to the altar of St. Sebastian, where an olive-skinned Italian boy tinkled a bell at the Consecration. Just beyond the vast square of St. Peter's they breakfasted at the restaurant of St. Peter and made plans for the campaign. With Father French and Father McGrath, their own Glenmarians who were studying in Rome, they called on Father Skeehan, the Dominican Procurator General. As his title indicated, he represented the Dominican Order in conducting its business with the Holy See. Father Garde, the Prior, arranged a meeting with Monsignor Spozetti of the Sacred Congregation of Religious. Father Sauvage, a Dominican, who had lived in the United States, discussed their mission with the Glenmary priests. He offered to see Monsignor Spozetti before the prearranged meeting and to show him the letters Father Bishop carried from the American Bishops. Both Father Bishop and Father Sourd were elated, but Father Skeehan warned them that in Rome patience was a necessary virtue.

On Sunday both missioners said Mass at the Dominican Church of Santa Maria. The only Gothic church in Rome, it rises above the ancient temple of Minerva, the pagan goddess of wisdom. Father Sourd sacrificed at the main altar above the tomb of St. Catherine of Siena. Nearby stood Michelangelo's famous Christ with the Cross, commemorating the legend which tells of Christ stopping Peter as he fled from Rome with the age-old query: "Quo vadis?" As Father Bishop walked back to the sacristy he stood before the questioning figure of Christ and wondered, "Where am I going?" He was in the city of Peter, in the hands of the Church. If God willed it, his Society would become a militant arm of His Church, approved by the Successor of Peter. He had no doubt that ultimately such would be the case. If the Roman prelates decided the time was not ripe for such a permanent step, he would return to his missioners to build further and to try again.

Tuesday came, the day of the meeting. The two American

priests bought the broad-brimmed, low-crowned hats of the Italian clergy, and wearing their cassocks, walked to the new building of the Sacred Congregation of Religious. The city awed them. In Vatican City, clerics in brilliant colors hurried past. Their own guide, Father Garde, the Dominican Prior, wore his spotless white robe. With him they arrived at the office of Monsignor Spozetti, the Secretary of the Congregation. He was not a bureaucrat, such as Father Bishop had sometimes met in his early lobbying days in Washington. On the contrary, the Monsignor greeted them graciously and put them at ease, talking of Rome and the Americans he knew, especially Archbishop McNicholas, whom he had admired years ago when the Archbishop was assistant to the Master General of the Dominicans in Rome. He listened with interest to the story of the Home Missioners, commenting on the wide areas of priestless counties in America, and especially on the information center at West Portsmouth, which was a new approach to him. He told them that all members of the Congregation agreed that the Society of the Home Missioners was a useful and necessary adjunct to the Church in the United States. Father Bishop merited the admiration and encouragement of the Holy See.

A difficulty had arisen, however. Archbishop McNicholas had requested the Sacred Congregation to grant a "Decree of Praise" to the Home Missioners of America, a diocesan society which he had erected, so that papal approval could follow. But the rules of the Congregation required that before a bishop could erect a diocesan society he had to consult the Congregation and obtain approval. This he had not done. A decree of erection had been issued before the Sacred Congregation had been given an opportunity to investigate the need for such a society. Consequently, the Congregation had not issued a *nihil obstat,* which the Archbishop should have obtained before he issued his official decree of erection. For that reason, tentatively, the Congregation had concluded no such diocesan society as the Home Missioners of America existed. The Monsignor held out hopes that the canonists might find a way out of these technical difficulties as no one desired to stop the growth of a Society deemed necessary by so many of the hierarchy of the United States. In any event a decision would be reached in five days.

Father Bishop listened attentively. This was a new and wholly unexpected obstacle. Certainly the Congregation would ratify the acts of the Archbishop; but the Society sought papal approval and that now appeared to be a request to be granted only after the Congregation had corrected an initial error. To obtain papal approval under those circumstances would be doubly difficult.

Father Bishop inquired directly to the point: "If the decision recognizes our Society as one of diocesan rite, can we hope for a Decree of Praise?" The Monsignor replied that ordinarily the Congregation was reluctant to give a *Decretum Laudis* unless the Society had at least a hundred clerics. That problem, however, had not been considered in view of the more pressing question as to whether or not the Home Missioners had a present legal existence.

Father Bishop left graciously, but worried. His political training in Washington, where he had sought approval of his farm rehabilitation project, stood him in good stead. Laws could not be broken, but they could always be interpreted. Of one thing he was certain, the Congregation informally approved of his Society. A path to a formal recognition had to be found through friends of Archbishop McNicholas, who were legion in Rome. As a young Dominican, Father McNicholas had spent five years in Rome as assistant to the Master of the Dominicans. He was remembered in the Roman Curia as a brilliant, holy person. He was known from his work in America as a loyal, militant son of the Holy Father.

Father Bishop recalled his "missionary shopping" among the bishops of America. "Approval shopping" might be handled in much the same manner. He called on Archbishop Pasetto of the Congregation of the Religious, who assured him a way would be found. He visited Cardinal Fumasoni-Biondi of the Propagation of the Faith, whom he had met in Baltimore when that Prelate was the Papal Delegate. The Cardinal told him he would personally see Cardinal Rossi of the Holy Office, who was a brilliant scholar in Church Law, and who highly respected Archbishop McNicholas.

The Dominican, Father Skeehan, took him to Monsignor Carboni of the papal household. Here was a skillful friend. There were two courses of action he advised. Let Father Bishop take the Archbishop's letter to Monsignor Montini, the assistant Papal Secretary of State, and with it his own very colorful explanation of the work of the Home Missioners. The Monsignor would help. At the same time arrange for an audience with the Holy Father. "Suggest to Monsignor Montini that a letter from His Holiness, either personally or through his Secretary, blessing your work will be as much help to you as a decree of praise from the Sacred Congregation of Religious. If you have further difficulties," he said, "don't hesitate to call me."

Several days later Monsignor Spozetti called to arrange a conference. The canonists had found an answer to the technical difficulties. The erection by the Archbishop of the Home Missioners as a Society of diocesan rite had been premature. However, the Congregation now had all the facts and if a *nihil obstat* had been sought by the Archbishop prior to erecting the Society, it would have been granted. Under those circumstances the required action could be made retroactive. Hence the Congregation would issue a decree validating and confirming the erection of the Home Missioners of America as a diocesan society. The Monsignor, himself, would rewrite the Constitution to give the Society as broad powers as were possible under Canon Law. However, no Decree of Praise to be followed by Pontifical approval could be granted, since the Society had less than fifty clerics. The Monsignor pointed out that this in itself was a concession as the Congregation normally required one hundred clerics before giving a *decretum laudis*. Until the Society grew and obtained such approval, it would remain under the jurisdiction of the Archbishop of Cincinnati.

Apparently the matter was concluded, but Father Bishop had heard Archbishop McNicholas say that in 1216 when St. Dominic asked the Holy See for approval of his Institute he had but sixteen members. Perhaps Monsignor Carboni might be able to suggest a step in the direction of full papal approval. That Prelate was not convinced that reconsideration was impossible. The Society now had twenty priests and five Brothers, just half the required number. If the Archbishop of Cincinnati considered it essential that a *decretum laudis* be given, perhaps the Congregation might make a further concession. At least, he said, the effort should be made. He advised Father Bishop to cable the Archbishop, informing him of the developments, and suggesting a renewed request by wire. That cable Father Bishop composed and sent at once.

The year 1947 was not the Holy Year for pilgrimages to Rome, but the Superior of the Home Missioners was certainly a pilgrim. He decided to visit the seven pilgrimage churches of Rome, praying for success, if that were the will of God.

In his diary we read: "Pilgrimage intention: That we may become more worthy of the favor we ask, Pontifical approval, if God sees fit; and that, if granted, we may never abuse the favor."

The pilgrimage was made on foot. It began at St. Peter's, where the four Glenmary priests knelt in adoration, oblivious of the masterpieces of the greatest artists of the Renaissance.

After crossing the Square of St. Peter's they walked miles to St. Paul Outside-the-Walls. Arriving there, Father Sourd and the two younger priests urged their Superior to sit in a cane-seated chair, while all of them prayed for the help of the first and greatest Missioner. The magnificence of the high altar, shaded by a gem-inlaid canopy and supported by four enormous columns of alabaster, in a small way represented the power of God, who would, if that were His will, answer their prayers. Close by, and outside the walls, they entered the Church of St. Sebastian, the third of the pilgrimage churches. Then, his feet aching, Father Bishop walked three miles to the mother and head of all churches, St. John Lateran, founded by the Emperor Constantine. Not far away was the fifth of the pilgrimage churches, Santa Croce, originally built by St. Helena to house a portion of the true cross. The last mile led them to the Church of San Lorenzo, partly destroyed by a bomb in the great war, and then to the Basilica of St. Mary Major where the pilgrims implored the help of Our Lady.

Several days later Father Bishop talked to Monsignor Montini, the assistant Papal Secretary of State, who is now the Cardinal Archbishop of Milan. Of slight build, serious and ascetic, he was gracious and friendly. He characterized the Society's work as "beautiful" and asked for the brochure which Father Bishop had prepared to show to the Holy Father.

That night Father Skeehan, the Procurator General of the

Dominicans, called. He had talked to Monsignor Spozetti, who had informed him that the Cardinal Administrator of the Congregation of Religious felt that the whole matter should be transferred to a new commission appointed to consider secular institutes under a recent constitution of the Holy Father, termed "Provida Mater Ecclesia," which had been issued on the Feast of the Purification of the Blessed Virgin, February 2, 1947, just four months previously.

No English translation was available. Father McCarthy of Cincinnati, residing at the Maryknoll House, hurriedly prepared one. Apparently, it provided for the organization of secular institutes as distinguished from religious institutes or societies that could be organized and approved under canons then existing. Like most new statute laws it required interpretation. In fact, on March 25, 1947, the Cardinal Prefect of the Congregation of Religious had appointed a special commission of jurists to interpret, apply, and complement the papal ruling where necessary. One of the jurists was Father Suarez, the Master General of the Dominicans. Father Skeehan was of the opinion that "Provida Mater Ecclesia" intended the organization of societies of secular priests without vows which, unlike religious groups, would not be obliged to live a community life. He advised that under "Provida Mater Ecclesia" the Congregation of Religious could set up and approve the Home Missioners as such a secular society. In fact, if Father Bishop followed that pattern, his Society might well be the first to be set up in America as such an organization with papal approval.

Father Bishop thought otherwise. Years ago he had modeled his Society after the Sulpicians and the Maryknoll rule. To him history demonstrated forcibly that most of the notably successful mission movements were performed by missioners working in groups, like well-organized mobile teams. Archbishop McNicholas, a skilled canonist himself, had erected the Community under Canon Law as a diocesan society, and this had happened prior to the "Provida Mater Ecclesia." Jurists were notoriously slow in arriving at decisions and a year might elapse before they could determine the status of his Society.

Father Bishop insisted that an immediate consultation with Monsignor Spozetti was necessary. So, unannounced, the two Glenmary priests from Cincinnati visited the Monsignor, who explained that he, too, had many doubts, which could only be resolved after the Commission had met. Possibly the jurists might agree with Father Bishop. At that moment Father Bishop made a decision. He could not wait. A commission of jurists, interpreting a wholly new concept, might take months and months before reaching his case. Better by far was it to accept what he could get now. "Isn't it a fact," he said, "that the Congregation of Religious will issue a ruling validating the Home Missioners as a Society of Diocesan Rite, and curing any defects that now exist?" The Monsignor answered in the affirmative, but he said: "I know both you and Archbishop McNicholas would like to get pontifical approval, and that is impossible at this time, unless you decide to follow the pattern set up by the Holy Father." Father Bishop answered: "If it please Your Excellency, let your ruling validating the Home Missioners be issued and, if God wills, our Society will grow and in a few years we will be back."

Nothing further could be done. A few days later he and Father Sourd had a personal audience with His Holiness, Pope Pius XII. He was well acquainted with the rural areas of America and promised his blessing would be sent officially to the new Society.

On June 18, 1947, the Archbishop of Cincinnati was authorized by the Sacred Congregation of Religious to approve by pontifical authority the Home Missioners of America as a diocesan institute. It was typical of the humility of His Grace, Archbishop McNicholas, that he suggested to Father Bishop that *The Challenge* carry an explanation. We read in the Summer Challenge of 1947:

"The Holy See in its Decree authorized the Ordinary of Cincinnati to validate by pontifical authority any or all acts that may have been defective in organizing the Society from the beginning and to state that this concession was granted by the Sacred Congregation of Religious."

On February 18, 1948, through Monsignor Montini, the Holy Father imparted his special Apostolic blessing to the priests, Brothers, students, and Sisters of the Society of the Home Missioners of America.

CHAPTER 10

ON HIS return from Rome Father Bishop published "A Glenmary Reverie" in the summer *Challenge*. He wrote with a nostalgic sweetness of the slanting hillsides and the picturesque fields of the mission areas. He stressed again that his central thought had always been to supply a need for the Church of Christ in the unfavored regions of America. His love of the soil was sharpened by the month he had lived in densely populated Rome. Week after week he drove to Otway, Ohio, or to the mission at Pond Creek saying his Sunday Masses in the mission churches. With Father Borchers he participated in the outdoor meeting at the village of Friendship, where a real crowd for that hamlet, seventy-five persons, stood in the warm clear air of a summer evening to hear the missioners talk of the existence of God and man's relation to Him. The immensity of the basilicas of Rome seemed small in the vast expanse of a clear sky, studded with stars.

Awaiting him at his desk was a picture of new St. Patrick's Chapel at Dunganon, Virginia, sent by Father Dean. Made of logs from trees felled in the surrounding forests, it was a blockhouse church with three gables, each surmounted by a cross. In it the spark of faith which had never died, was being rekindled in a score of Irish Catholics, who had proudly hewn and shaped the logs in a labor of love for their own good St. Patrick.

On his desk were letters from His Excellency Emmet W. Walsh, Bishop of Charleston, who offered Williamsburg County in South Carolina as the sixth mission area of the Glenmary Fathers. In September of 1947 Father Patrick Quinlan, an aspirant Home Missioner, took up residence in a two-room cottage at Kingstree, close to St. Anne's Church, where never before had there been a resident pastor. The forty Catholics among a population of forty thousand in the county knew once again that their Church of St. Anne would be open every day of their lives.

Father Sourd went back to his trailer chapel to become a gypsy priest. In small hamlets, as he stood on the platform, his cassock whipping in the wind, his hand steadying the microphone, he told quaint stories to the farmers gathered around, each tale a home-spun illustration of a Catholic truth.

From Russellville and Sunfish, Kentucky, came enthusiastic letters from the young missioners. Father Wuest wrote with pardonable pride that in Butler County, near Sunfish, his flock consisted of three Catholic families, well instructed in the Faith. Father Dean wrote from Norton, Virginia, that he had given Holy Communion to four prisoners on a road gang near the Tennessee border. From Statesboro, Georgia, Father Smith invited the Superior to see the store he had converted into a chapel. He described the handmade canopy over the altar, noting that it was liturgically correct.

The summer passed with intermittent visits to doctors, promotional trips to Chicago and the East, lectures to the students, and a few Sundays of relaxation in the Ohio mission areas. In the autumn, before his annual visitation to the missions, Father Bishop cast up the score of his Society. Under his immediate supervision were sixteen ordained priests and five Brothers. Undergoing at least a partial missionary training were five clerical students in theology and four in philosophy. In addition, ten students pledged to the Society were in major and minor seminaries, and seventeen young women comprised the women's group. In all he could count a grand total of sixty-one persons, either working in the mission regions of America or anxiously awaiting the days of adventure in the mission fields.

For two weeks in the fall Father Bishop visited the six mission areas in the South. He found the work forging ahead with slow but steady gains. In Sunfish, the first of his hidden villages, he took morning walks along the narrow gravel roads, greeting some of the three hundred devout Catholics who now asked for, and obtained, the maximum in religious services at their own St. John's parish. At Morgantown he prayed in the frame cottage mission chapel, where twice a month twenty Catholics, all baptized within the past two years, heard Mass. In Russellville, three Glenmary Sisters introduced him in the new school to their twenty-eight pupils. One little eight-year-old, carefully coached by Sister Mary Francis wrote on the blackboard: "Welcome to Father Bishop." The years of effort had not been wasted.

At Guthrie, a Russellville mission, he found Father Healy visiting his small flock of twenty Catholics. They had no church, heard Mass in a private home, and talked of the day when a chapel would be built.

When Father Bishop had visited Statesboro a year earlier the mission center, with its backdrop of shade trees, was flourishing. Now it was burned to the ground. A store, converted into a chapel, was a temporary substitute. Father Smith spoke enthusiastically of a new brick church he hoped to build. To Father Bishop plans and drawings of churches and chapels had always offered a deep satisfaction. He loved them. He spent hours with Father Smith, praising some details, suggesting changes in others. He knew Statesboro flourished in good hands.

At Kingstree, South Carolina, he found Father Quinlan living in a two-room tourist cottage as happy and proud as if he owned all of Williamsburg County. The words of the Roman Breviary flashed in his mind:

> "Lift up thine eyes, O Jerusalem, and see
> the power of thy King; behold the Savior
> cometh to free thee from bondage."

In Norton, Virginia, he spent an evening at St. Anthony's recreation hall, recently moved to its new cinder block gymnasium, where the youth of Norton and Wise County came to play ping-pong and basketball and to sing around the upright piano.

In Otway, Ohio, he examined the plans of Father Borchers for his new mission church at West Portsmouth. He said Mass at St. Ann-by-the-Wayside in Buena Vista. This was his kingdom — these hills and valleys. These were his people. Slowly, so slowly, but in God's good time, with his little black army of priests and Brothers, and his little gray army of Sisters, he was bringing to the suspicious mountaineers, the frustrated sharecroppers, the toilers and the miners a share of the charity God had promised them.

The year 1948 was a trying time for Father Bishop. His own community of men now was a moral entity. Although under the supervision of Archbishop McNicholas, its permanency could be affected only by the authority of the Pope himself. In his plan, the Sisters of the home missions at some time had to be established as an autonomous separate entity under a Constitution which would obligate them to work in the rural missions of America.

He realized that in their years of preparation the Sisters had to be fostered and held together as a unit by the Archbishop. From the beginning Father Bishop had interviewed and accepted applicants. He had prescribed their training in religion and had arranged courses in social sciences, backed up by practical nursing experience in hospitals. If they were to contribute to the realization of his ideals, they had to be prepared specially for the missions. At the same time they had to be religious of the Church, having a precise knowledge of religious life and its practices. This latter need was foremost to Archbishop McNicholas. In supplying it, he had enlisted first the aid of the Dominican Sisters of Columbus, and then the Dominican Sisters of Adrian, Michigan. Under their tutelage the practices of the Third Order of St. Dominic formed a basis for the religious life of the Community. Under the influence of Father Bishop their habit was gray, and not the spotless white of the Dominicans. As he visualized them, they were his gray army.

In 1948 he sensed that the Dominican Sisters and the Archbishop were not wholly in accord with him. He feared that a trend was growing to clothe the Sisters in white in their convent, and perhaps in gray only when in the mission field. He feared that if the trend persisted the Sisters would eventually lose at least a part of their autonomy, and this he considered would be disastrous to his plan. The Archbishop took the position that the Sisters were his spiritual responsibility and no definite decision concerning their future could be made at that time.

Father Bishop was certain of the course to be followed. He had never vacillated in his determination to build the Home Missioners, including the Sisters, exactly as he conceived them in his original plan published in the *Ecclesiastical Review*. He was a stubborn man in the sense that he would not acquiesce voluntarily to a change until he was certain God willed it. In his prayers he asked that his will be made subservient to what was pleasing to God. But he could see many obstacles in a co-operating community of Sisters, which might lose a part of its self rule through too close an affiliation with the Dominican Order. In the mission fields white habits would be out of place, and in the convent, the Sisters should be wholly Home Missioners and not Dominican Sisters. The purpose of the Community must be to labor in the mission rural areas, and to Father Bishop that aim had to dominate all its activities.

Father Bishop did not object to the rule of St. Dominic for his Sisters. But he feared that at some time they might be termed Dominican Sisters and not Sisters of the Home Missions. The Archbishop refused to discuss with him the ultimate religious form of the Community. As a good priest, Father Bishop took no active steps to thwart any purpose of the Archbishop. He waited and prayed that God might see fit to make his gray army a separate division of the militant arm of His Church.

In 1949 Archbishop McNicholas petitioned the Sacred Congregation of Religious at Rome for authority to erect the Sisters of the Home Missions as a separate society of diocesan rite, working in co-operation with the Home Missioners of America. Until the Society was erected, and its Constitution adopted and confirmed, no final decision could be made as to the extent of its affiliation with the Dominican Order. In the meantime, Father Bishop lectured the Sisters on missionary ideals and techniques, continued their training in social work — and prayed.

In 1948 Father Bishop was sixty-two years old. A rheumatic condition in his right arm would not yield to treatment and was to trouble him until his death. The early affliction of his spine had returned in a slight degree. But his good humor and cheerfulness expanded as the days followed one another, each one adding to the growth of his Society. His daily work became more varied and heavier than before. For three years he had dreamed of a new seminary and mother house. The plans as drawn by Edward Schulte, a Cincinnati architect, proposed an American colonial structure. As Father Bishop wrote: "The style is American because America is the scene of our labors." The building would face southeast toward the areas in which the Home Missioners had started their first missions. High above the center would rise a tower, surmounted by the cross.

Year by year construction had been delayed. By 1948 some sort of a new building was a necessity. The barracks, measuring thirty-five by seventy feet, housing the priests and the Brothers, and the hundred-year-old farmhouse, housing the Sisters were totally inadequate.

The original plans had called for an auxiliary low, one-story building, intended for a laundry, garage, and boiler room. Separate from the main building, consisting of two wings and a central chapel, the boiler house would contain all the utilities. From time to time, Father Bishop estimated the cost of one wing and the boiler house. The cost increased at each computation. The Society could not afford even one wing; but housing had to be provided for the growing Community, and a small seminary was essential. The lowly boiler house might do if it could take on a second story and the laundry and garage space be used for a tiny chapel, classrooms, and a refectory. With Edward Schulte, the architect, he made and fitted squares into a checkerboard until the Boiler-House Seminary emerged, capable of housing eighteen priests and students. On May 24, 1948, he broke ground, with Father Sourd standing at his shoulder. It marked the beginning of a more united existence, wherein the Fathers and the theological students could live together at Glenmary. Ready to teach were Father Marquardt and Father French, whom Father Bishop's foresight had sent to Rome to complete their studies. The former rural pastor of Clarksville, Maryland, showed a remarkable aptitude in planning broad outlines and working out the details so that, when finally accomplished, each project was always ready to be used.

With the Boiler-House Seminary completed in 1949 and the Barracks now housing the Sisters, other threads could be woven into the fabric of the Home Missioners. The hundred-year-old farmhouse became the home of the Novitiate. Remembering the promise of Bishop Walsh of the Maryknoll Fathers to train the first priests, Father Bishop requested a Maryknoll Father as the first Novice Master. Genial Father Francis MacRae came; in earlier days he had lived in the farmhouse with the first members of the Society. Father Bishop intended that at some time each member of the Society, including himself, should take the novice training. Above all technical missionary education he placed the necessity of a solid religious foundation. He knew that for those who entered a Society of the Church, a novitiate provided the means of acquiring a spirit of prayer and meditation. He once said that the life of a priest is a state of striving for perfection; that an active life, although necessary for a Home Missioner, must yield periodically to prayer, meditation, and reflection. We learn from his diary that when problems beset him, he turned to spiritual reading to lessen the impact of material tribulations.

In the first Novitiate there were two priests, four Brothers, and three students. All followed a rigorous schedule of prayer, meditation, manual labor, and recreation. Father MacRae, experienced as he was, conferred often with the founder. Some of his suggestions were adopted, others declined. Father Bishop had perfected a technique of sending up trial baloons and encouraging their deflation. It was a method by which he clarified his own thinking.

A training plan for the Glenmary Brothers began taking shape under the direction of Father Clement Borchers, now a veteran missioner. A five year program was gradually worked out in which courses in the spiritual life were balanced with the manual arts and crafts training to equip young men as competent mission companions for the Glenmary priests.

Since 1939 Father Bishop had prepared and edited the *Challenge*, writing at least one article in each number. As he described it on the masthead, it was a periodical of not too frequent occurrence, appearing at the four seasons of the year with no subscribers and no subscription rates. Always a journalist in the modern tradition, he knew the value of visual aids in arousing the interest of his readers. With the aid of the talented young priest artist, Father Patrick O'Donnell, he scoured the mission territory for snapshots, quaintly explaining the needs of his people, or illustrating the charitable work of the missioners and Sisters. Father Bishop's prose was terse and active. From time to time, he wrote as a teacher, urging that to establish the Kingdom of God men must have a true idea of what it is, not one perverted by ignorance or egotism. His missionary band, he wrote, must be spiritual supermen. Heaven must feel the unrelenting violence of their prayers, their self-denials, their daily meditations. The Sanctuary must know them as intimates.

CHAPTER 11

IN THE spring *Challenge* of 1950 Father Bishop noted the chief events of the preceding two years. One of his first "boys," Father Earl McGrath, had been killed in an automobile accident in Georgia and buried in "God's Half Acre" on the Glenmary grounds. Many recall Father Bishop's last stop at the fenced enclosure as he showed visitors about Glenmary. Invariably, he stood for a moment in silent prayer beside the grave. A human memory came to him of a black-cassocked young man in Rome, offering him a cane-seated chair in the Church of St. Paul Outside-the-Walls on that long pilgrimage when he sought divine help in his quest for papal approval. Under the Old Law God demanded of his people the first fruits of the harvest. Glenmary had given back to the Creator one of His first gifts.

Other events brought happier memories. In Virginia the mission territory had grown. Appalachia and two counties had been separated from the Norton area to become a new mission field with Father Raymond Dehen as its first pastor. In Russellville, Kentucky, a Christmas Crib was placed in the Court House Square, welcomed alike by Catholics and Protestants. It was a picturesque and novel religious expression to the Christians of that community. To Father Bishop it was the yearly miracle he loved — the rebirth of man's close relationship to his Creator. That was the season when the good Father with his own hands hung holly and pine branches about the chapel, and gave missals or perhaps a small volume of the *Imitation of Christ* to his friends. His eyes twinkled, his voice lightened at Christmas.

A new mission area of Bennettsville and Cheraw in South Carolina was opened. In June of 1949 Father Bishop preached at the dedication of the church in West Portsmouth, Ohio, and in September of the same year he turned that thriving parish back to Bishop Ready of Columbus. It was the first mission area developed by the Home Missioners to graduate from its "mission status" to be manned by a diocesan priest. It proved that Father Bishop's plan, first proposed in the May issue of the *Ecclesiastical Review*, to turn back mission parishes to the diocese when they became fully established, remained as a guiding principle.

The Norton Medical Clinic functioned as the first Catholic Hospital in the Virginia mission area. Months of planning and negotiations with the Sisters of the Poor Servants of the Mother of God had produced this modern rural miracle.

In the spring of 1950, on April 22, Archbishop McNicholas died. In his diary of that day, Father Bishop wrote: "The best friend of our Society has passed! What of the future?"

In the *Challenge* he wrote from his heart: "We of Glenmary feel deeply the favor of God's guiding hand in bringing us under the enlightened direction of so experienced, so wise, so learned and sympathetic a friend. He will hold in perpetuity a place of honor and affection in our Community's memory and, as in his lifetime, a place of highest importance in our prayers."

"What of the future?" wrote Father Bishop. The Archbishop died while important plans were being made. Much had been done under his direction. The Home Missioners had been established as a Society of secular priests in accordance with Canon Law. Missioners were in No-Priest-Land. But a permanent mother house and seminary had to be built — and the co-operating Sisterhood had to be set up canonically as a distinct Society. These were ends to be accomplished under a new Archbishop, who might or might not pick up the reins and guide the Society with the same fatherly care as his predecessor. As usual Father Bishop sought the assurance of his Master in the tabernacle. He prayed to solve each day's problems without undue fear of the future.

From the first of March he had sought permission to build at least one wing of the mother house. The Archbishop had been too ill to see him. After the death of Archbishop McNicholas, Bishop Rehring had been made diocesan administrator. Father Bishop hastened to make the same request. On Tuesday, May 4, while giving a class in religion to the Sisters, he was called to the phone. It was His Excellency, Bishop Rehring, who authorized him to let the contracts for building the left wing of the seminary. In anticipation, bids had been obtained from contractors two months before. Father Bishop was as jubilant as a child. He found no one in the Boiler House to whom he could tell the news. In his diary we read: "Notified Honnert, the successful bidder, by phone. He promises to start next Monday, May 8. It was such an eventful day that I called Father Sourd long distance in Dubuque, Iowa, about our permission to build."

In the summer the Archdiocese of Cincinnati opened its arms to its newly installed Archbishop, Karl J. Alter. Father Bishop found his new Superior had a deep love for missions and missionary activities. He recognized a kindred spirit in His Excellency, whose approach to the use of social service as the handmaid of missionary labors was the same as his own. The good Father had once written to his "boys": "Charity is the open sesame to the door of an unbeliever."

No word from Rome had come, approving of the Sisters' community as a separate diocesan society, but the trend toward a Dominican affiliation had weakened. Sister Kevin, who had molded the Community into a fine religious group, had returned to Adrian, Michigan, and Sister John Joseph, O.P., had replaced her. The Sisters took her to their hearts. Of the twenty-three Sisters now comprising the Community, eighteen had expressed themselves against Dominican affiliation. When so informed by Father Bishop, the Archbishop reserved comment until he had the opportunity of a personal visitation.

His sixty-four years had affected Father Bishop's physical movements. His Mass was somewhat slower, although throughout his priestly life his realization of the mystery of the Divine Sacrifice had caused him to linger over the liturgy. Mentally he moved swiftly and accurately. Not content with the multiple problems of a growing Society thrust upon him, he pondered on how to make Glenmary's work in the missions more effective. He spent hours on developing a book of prayers and religious exercises to be used by his people in the mission areas on the Sundays when Mass was not available to them. In block letters on his manuscript he termed it: "Services For the Far-a-Ways." He arranged with the Jesuit Novitiate at Milford, near Cincinnati, for the use of an old building, resembling his own first "Barracks," as the house for his novices. Every Sunday, when he could, he sat with the novices in their new home, talking to them of the sacrifices of the missionary's life, and the wide expanse of the untilled fields of America awaiting their hands. With the approval of Archbishop Alter he worked out financing plans for his seminary. He made his annual visitation to the missions, finding renewed inspiration in the statistics of more baptisms, more conversions, and more children in the catechetical classes of the Sisters.

Nor did he forget in his annual "midwinter letter" to his associates his insistence on the growth of the inner spiritual life. He wrote: "May it not be well for each of us to make choice of a daily practice for our Society: the sanctification of our members, the success of our works, adequate vocations, our benefactors living and dead — something in addition to the four Masses offered monthly by our priests and the weekly Communions of our Sisters and Brothers? But may we not, also, as a personal observance, set aside some daily pious practice? God will certainly bless us if we do. And if we are constantly attentive to the improvement of the inner life of the spirit, God will see to it that our prayers for the great enterprise for which He has called us will be answered beyond our expectations. If our interior life is not kept on a high plane, our work can have only an apparent success and that not for very long. The fundamental requirement for true success is that all of us strive daily to be saints."

Since 1948 Father Bishop had drafted and redrafted the Constitution for his Society. In that year he had received a skeletal instrument from Rome, written in Italian. Weaving his own ideas about it, he had broadened its scope to the point where he could consult Archbishop McNicholas. Unfortunately, the Archbishop had been too ill to go over the document. In 1951, Father Bishop felt the Constitution was ready for approval. With the aid of Father McCarthy, Secretary to Archbishop Alter, some changes were made and the final draft submitted to the Archbishop. Again numerous changes were made by His Excellency who considered every word of it with meticulous care. Finally on March 29, 1951, Archbishop Alter gave his written approval to the permanent Constitution.

As provided therein, a General Chapter had to be convoked to elect a Superior General. At the initial meeting twelve electors would take part. These would be Father Bishop, the Superior pro-tem, four general councilors appointed by the Archbishop, the House Superior, and six other priests of the Society who had taken the perpetual oath. These latter would have to be elected by all the members who had taken the perpetual oath. So far the oaths had been of a temporary nature.

On Sunday, August 26, 1951, at the end of a retreat of seven days, the proceedings preliminary to the convocation of the first Chapter began. Gathered in the chapel of the Novitiate at Milford, the priests sang the "Veni Creator" while the Blessed Sacrament, in splendid isolation, dominated the altar. After Benediction a jubilant "Te Deum" rang through the open windows. Then Father Sourd, delegated by the Archbishop, administered the perpetual oath to Father Bishop, who on bended knee promised to consecrate himself for all of his life to the work of the missions committed to the Society. In turn, the Superior gave the same oath to Father Sourd and eleven of the priests. Father Bishop wrote in his diary: "It was a wonderful day. At long last we have received the accolade of the Church as her chosen knights."

On Monday, August 27, in the former Jesuit Retreat House at Milford, Archbishop Alter presided over the election of the six priests, who with the four councilors, the Novitiate House Superior, and Father Bishop would constitute the Chapter. On Tuesday, after a solemn Mass in honor of the Holy Spirit, the Chapter met. Father Bishop was elected Superior General for a six-year term. In the very words of the Constitution Father Bishop prayed that God, who had placed this burden upon him, would also help him carry it, for He was both the Author of the duty and the Giver of the grace to fulfill it.

In his 1951 annual letter to the missioners in the field Father Bishop stated, perhaps better than he had ever done before, his "credo" of a missioner. He wrote:

"The work of making converts is the missioner's prime object, and I do not in the least desire to weaken his efforts for this purpose. It is in perfect accord with the Savior's injunction to 'teach and baptize,' and it must ever be our chief objective.

"But I am convinced that side by side with the great convert-making purpose, there is another objective for us to cherish in our work. That objective is to lift up and improve the moral lives of the people around us, regardless of their beliefs or lack of beliefs; regardless, even, whether they will ever accept the Faith or not.

"We have been telling them what they must do now and every day in order to deserve anything of God. We have been holding up before them the treasured beliefs of full-fledged Catholicity as the cure for their spiritual ailments, although it may take years for them to accept them by an Act of Faith. At the same time, we have been withholding from them the first-aid package of the Commandments, the virtues, the duty of prayer — which can help them even now — by strengthening their sincerity, improving their lives and drawing down graces that can lead eventually to conversion.

"By doing this you are accomplishing two things. First you are broadcasting to them a message of daily conduct which is in line with the teaching of Christ. Second, you are drawing into the ambit of Catholic moral practice people who look for strong guidance and inspiration from a truly God-sent messenger."

CHAPTER 12

EARLY in 1952 Father Bishop conceived a plan to take the same training as his novices for a six-month period at the Novitiate in Milford. He consulted his confessor, who gave his approval. His Holiness Benedict XV wrote in 1921 that the noviceship was instituted to train the souls of novices in the extirpation of evil ways, the restraint of the passions, the acquisition of virtues, and the practice of the regular life; so that they may learn to make progress toward Christian perfection, which constitutes the end of every religious.

Father Bishop was sixty-six years old and a deeply spiritual priest. Of necessity he had hewn a path through every obstacle, and in the process he realized more than anyone else that success had hardened his will, that at times his pride made him reluctant to accept opposition. In his intimate conversations with his own personal God he first rationalized his actions and then with utter humility prayed that God would help him suppress these appraisals of his own importance. If he could humble himself to accept the complete obedience demanded of a novice, perhaps he could make greater progress toward the Christian perfection which he sought.

His lay friends considered him a charming Southern gentleman, a man who took lightly the honors that life had given him. Inwardly he was in constant conflict. As a man of action in ordering the affairs of his Community, he often demanded obedience as a matter of right rather than on a rational basis. In his examination of his own conscience, he questioned his integrity. After the Council was formed, he found himself resenting requests for more detailed information. In his prayers he ascribed these human failings to the work of the devil and humbly sought the gift of humility.

In the novitiate Father Bishop worked with his hands as any other novice, scrubbing floors, washing dishes, polishing candlesticks. Labor on the paths around the Barracks he had to forego as arthritis in both arms and stiffness in his spine made it difficult for him. Even light work caused such pain that he was compelled to take diathermy treatments at St. Mary's Hospital.

On December 8, the feast of Our Lady, in the middle of a thirty-day retreat, which ended his novice training, he wrote a prayer, laden with his own inner conflict. He wrote: "Dear Blessed Mother, sanctify this retreat for me and obtain that I garner from it all the graces needed to overcome my stubborn vices, and to develop strong virtues in their place, and particularly that I become a Superior General to thine own liking."

The spring of 1952 saw the completion and dedication of the Glenmary Seminary and Mother House. Five bishops and many priests participated. Archbishop Alter wrote: "If the indefatigable zeal, the humility and the drive of the founder and the first priests and Sisters of the Home Missioners are to be typical of the young men who will answer the challenge to help make rural America Catholic, and fill your seminary in the future, then the Home Missioners, with God's grace, will not fail. May the crown of your Society be a harvest of souls in rural America."

In the Spring *Challenge* the Home Missioners rejoiced. Father Bishop reported that the members totaled twenty-three priests, twelve Brothers, fifty-six students, and thirty-five Sisters. Fourteen years of work and prayer had accomplished a modern miracle.

There was little resemblance between the hundred-year-old farmhouse of 1940, the Barracks of 1941, the Boiler House of 1949, and this new, sturdy seminary building; yet each had been a milestone on the way to maturity. In the hinterland, the mission chapels and churches overshadowed the home base. From the tiny parishes came photographs of rugged America with equally rugged missioners and gentle-ministering Sisters. As the editor of the *Challenge,* Father Bishop found in these pictures a sermon more instructive than any he could preach.

While Father Bishop trained with his novices, the final stone was placed in the broad base of the plan he had published in 1936 in the *Ecclesiastical Review.* On July 16, 1952, Archbishop Alter issued a decree constituting and establishing "The Home Mission Sisters of America" as a Congregation of Religious women of diocesan rite. At the same time he approved a Constitution, in which the Sisters proclaimed themselves an entity, unaffiliated with any other Order or Society. The Rule adopted for their religious practices was that of St. Augustine. Side by side, as foreseen by their founder, the Home Mission Sisters and Glenmary Missioners each had a moral entity, according to Canon Law, and each was destined to leave a heritage of mission victories for all the missioners who would follow them.

With the completion of the first phase of his work, Father Bishop faced the future with a realization of the immensity of the task before his Society. But the thought comforted him. God had intended that every man leave some good behind him on which others could build. It was in the Divine Plan that he, William Howard Bishop, should die, but others, perhaps worthier than he would carry on and because of his accomplishments would speed all the faster to the goal for which his Society was founded. Echoing these thoughts he wrote in the *Challenge:* "It is America's task — who can say it is not her providential assignment — to save and rescue the world. This being the case, Glenmary is now at work in the most important strategic position in the world. We are laboring for the spiritual rescue of the nation that must rescue the world. In our work we have no illusions as to the magnitude of the labors that confront us. It will be a task of many years, certainly of many generations."

CHAPTER 13

IN 1953, for the first year in its history, Glenmary knew the quiet routine of community life untouched by groaning bulldozers and the tapping of carpenters' hammers. At 5:30 A.M. the priests, students, and Brothers rose, and at 6:30 Father Bishop said the Community Mass before a crucifix which he himself had chosen. The high arched windows on both sides of the chapel looked across the pleasant fields of Glenmary. The cost of the chapel had been borne by Mr. & Mrs. Thomas Bradley of New York City. The Bradleys, as true missioners, had now erected a chapel on every continent of the Globe.

In his inner spiritual life the good priest was closer to contentment than ever before. His diary, while a factual account of his daily activities, rarely noted any spiritual complacency. Yet on Saturday, January 3, 1953, we read: "During recent weeks I have had a deeper and steadier consolation in prayer — more so than ever before or during my entire priestly life. I love to visit the Manger and meditate on the unbelievable harmony between the eternal majesty of God and His self-effacing humility in the person of Christ."

In his busy schedule Father Bishop now found time to rewrite a pamphlet he termed "Services for the Far-aways." In March he accepted a new mission territory from the Bishop of Oklahoma. With Monsignor Harkin of the Oklahoma Diocese he drove to St. Joseph's, the base parish in Buffalo, Oklahoma, and to the mission church in Shattuck, the largest town in Ellis County. In the two sections were fifteen thousand people. Twenty-five Catholic families formed the congregation in Buffalo and fifteen in Shattuck. Father Marquardt characterized his parishioners as truly of the West, proud of their town, proud of their State, and above all proud that they were Catholics. As he drove along the wide open spaces of wheat and cattle country, Father Bishop mentally noted that two more counties of No-Priest-Land, U.S.A., would soon be removed from the black areas of the Home Missioners' Map.

Shortly afterward, Archbishop Alter consented to administer the sacrament of holy orders in Glenmary's own chapel. Four of the theologians, previously tested in the crucible of the Novitiate, were scheduled to be ordained. On May 17 a bright sun poured through the clean, slender chapel windows while the Archbishop spread oil on the hands of the initiates and bade them receive the Holy Spirit and offer the ancient sacrifice of God's own body. The mother house had earned its name. Father Bishop, and beside him Father Sourd, knelt to kiss the dedicated palms of these young missioners, who in turn gave a blessing to their Superiors. If Father Bishop's eyes grew moist it could be ascribed only to the joy he felt that these physically strong young men had promised their lives to bring Christian charity to the spiritually starved men and women in America's hills and backlands.

In the early days at Clarksville Father Bishop had enlisted the aid of a Catholic women's group. In Cincinnati he had found Catholic women equally co-operative. They were the little mothers who mended and embroidered vestments, and somehow were instrumental in raising funds when other sources dried up. Each year the Glenmary Guild of Women planned and held a benefit dinner on Laetare Sunday. In 1953 Monsignor Quinn, a friend of the missions, acted as toastmaster. He described eloquently the work of Father Bishop and his missioners. The thousand men and women at the dinner went away each with a feeling that they had a part in a great work of their century.

On May 22, 1953, the annual visitation of the Superior General began. Father Kelly, the Treasurer General, accompanied him. No one knew better than Father Bishop that proper accounting in a rural parish was even more necessary than in a city parish. He remembered well the days at Clarksville when setting up the budget and later balancing it needed more than a bookkeeper. In Russellville, Kentucky, the first stop, he suggested to the mission pastor, Father Healy, with a twinkle in his eye, that Father Kelly in a few hours could solve not only his accounting problems but his financial ones as well. The next day Father Healy took them to a new church under construction at Franklin, Kentucky. It had a few financial worries of its own but, as Father Bishop knew, God could and would provide. Eleven years before, in one room in a dwelling in this very town a Home Missioner had offered Mass for six Catholics. Today there were eighty parishioners, anxious to worship in their new Church of St. Mary, then being built of their native stone.

On Pentecost Sunday Father Bishop sang High Mass at St. John's Church in Sunfish, Kentucky. He preached on the guiding spirit of the Holy Ghost in the spread of the Church. In the afternoon he umpired a ball game — "School Boys" versus "Old Men." It was disconcerting to find his youthful and vigorous missioner, Father Boland, forty years younger than himself, among the "Old Men."

Statesboro, Georgia, was the next stopping place, reached

by plane from Bowling Green, Kentucky, to Savannah, and then by car on a hot and dusty road. With Father Nagele, Father Bishop and Father Kelly sat on the rectory lawn in the moonlight, chatting of the Polish emigrants whom Father Ed Smith had introduced to Georgia rural life, and who slowly but surely had migrated to the big cities. The next day the Superior General made his routine examination of the books. He was much more interested in Father Nagele's idea of a mission project in certain Negro settlements near Statesboro.

Two days later he returned to Glenmary, tired from the long drive, but facing a schedule in which there was no time for rest. On Saturday, May 30, with Father Sourd he drove to West Union, Ohio. Both priests were in a reminiscent mood. They recalled the first evening services in West Union, thirteen years before, when a group of objectors trained a powerful flashlight on Father Bishop as he spoke to forty or fifty townfolk. The next night he returned with two subdeacons. An American sense of fair play and respect for courage enabled him to speak without interruption — his topic, "Forgiveness of Sin." Those were cherished recollections of high adventure. Tomorrow in this town the first permanent chapel in Adams County, Holy Trinity Church, would be dedicated by Archbishop Alter.

Against a backdrop of rugged, eroded hills the Home Missioners, under the direction of Father William Smith, had built in West Union a chapel in Colonial style with a bell tower, surmounted by a slender steeple and the cross of Christ. A roofed porch, upheld by four columns, sheltered the inviting double doors of the church entrance. A long community hall of the same construction formed a right angle to the chapel. Here would be a mission base where families could worship at the altar, and within the shadow of the church gather for innocent amusement and relaxation.

The next morning, Sunday, May 31, Father Bishop served the Dedication Mass of Archbishop Alter. The splendid liturgy of the Church somehow magnified that small chapel. The Churches of Rome could be no more brilliant.

CHAPTER 14

ON TUESDAY, June 2, 1953, after working at his desk in the morning, Father Bishop left Glenmary for the last time. He was sixty-seven years of age, in fair health and anxious to complete his visitation of the Virginia missions. On Friday evening with Brother Robert, who drove the car, he arrived at St. Anthony's Church in Norton. After going over the work of the mission with Father Dehen, on Saturday he zigzagged to the top of High Knob over a narrow gravel road, which on his first visit he had termed a "jittery highway." The ridges were green and gold in the sun while the mountain streams below still frothed from the May showers. Uphill and downhill he drove, along Big Stoney Creek, a picturesque collection of perhaps five mountain cabins, and then to Hunter's Valley, where he was met by Father Bob Berson. The clean air of the mountains invigorated him. In the deepening twilight he visited Christ the King Chapel, built mostly by the hands of Father Berson and his small group of parishioners. It was much like a barn with two windows on each side, but the door was open and at the rustic altar a sanctuary lamp burned. Father Bishop remembered a day in the fall after the sorghum had ripened, when the mountain folk gathered together to grind the stems of the sweet sorgo, and in a common kettle to boil the juice until it thickened into a viscous syrup. Brother Charles, one of his first Brothers, and then living in his own cabin among the mountain people, had spread it, thick and warm, on a slab of whole wheat bread and offered it to him.

He slept well that night. On Sunday he said the late Mass, as he always did in every mission church. In the last sermon of his life he explained the meaning of the Divine Sacrifice. Was it a mere coincidence that in his first priestly resolution twenty-six years before, Father Bishop had written: "I will endeavor to make the Mass my chief preoccupation and care, the center of my religious life. I will preach frequently on the sublime Sacrifice, this with the help of Almighty God and His Divine Son, whom it is my privilege to receive and offer daily."

On Monday, June 8, he drove to Sacred Heart Church in Appalachia, where Father Francis Wuest, the pastor, had engaged a Passionist Father to give a mission to his congregation of coal miners and their families. In the evening after the mission sermon Father Bishop raised the Blessed Sacrament in Benediction. Later he knelt before the Sacred Heart Shrine at a side altar, reading his office.

The next morning he said the last Mass of his life. A coal-laden train rumbled as usual along the tracks within fifty feet of the altar.

After breakfast a sharp pain in his chest caused him to remark to Father Wuest: "That's a new one for me, Father." As the pain continued Dr. Gordon Shull, the local physician, was called. He ordered him taken by ambulance to St. Mary's Hospital in Norton, eleven miles away. As he left the rectory on a stretcher, he told Father Wuest to follow him, saying, "Bring your parish books with you; we'll finish the visitation at the hospital. It'll be a very quiet place."

Father Wuest obediently placed the books in his car and drove to Norton. When he arrived there, Sister Mary Patrice, the Superior of the hospital, informed him that Father Bishop was resting comfortably. He could receive visitors for a short period. As Father Wuest entered the room, Father Bishop said: "Did you bring the books?" "Yes," the missioner replied, "but they tell me the doctors . . ." "Now, now, Father," his Superior interjected, "Appalachia is my last visitation; let's get on with it."

For fifteen minutes Father Bishop asked questions and checked the parish records. Then, relaxing against his bed pillows, he chatted in his drawling voice of affairs at Glenmary. Father Wuest was silent. He had learned from Sister Mary Patrice that his Superior had a very serious heart condition, and he wondered if the patient had been told. Father Bishop knew, but in his philosophy he welcomed life as a temporary gift of his Maker to be used in His service. If death were near, he would meet it smiling and working. Father Wuest wished to say the prayers for the sick. Doctor Tudor, a friend of the mission hospital of St. Mary, occupied at that time an adjoining room. Father Bishop, who knew him well, suggested that the young priest call on Doctor Tudor and then return.

Wednesday was quiet and comforting. Father Preske, one of Father Bishop's youngest priests, then assistant at Sacred Heart, Appalachia, brought him Holy Communion. All that day he rested, content to savor the joy of a long meditation, or the pleasure of a short nap, or the easy give and take of light conversation with the Sisters. In the evening Father Wuest and Glenmary's student priest, Father Joseph O'Donnell, who had just arrived from the Catholic University in Washington, visited him. He was in high spirits. Before they left, they laid their hands on his head and blessed him, and then, kneeling, they received his last blessing.

At four o'clock on Thursday morning, June 11, 1953, a

sharp attack made breathing difficult. He was placed in an oxygen tent. Father O'Donnell heard his confession and anointed him. At his bedside sat Brother Robert, his face downcast, his rosary flowing from his fingers. Father Bishop was the calmest man in the room. In a warm voice, perhaps a little weak, he said to the Brother: "Don't take it so hard. I'll be all right." A moment later when the Sister Superior came into the room, he raised his right hand against the transparent wall of the oxygen tent and smiled.

Two hours later, he died — suddenly. A Sister fell to her knees, whispered a prayer, and then turned off the oxygen.

On June 16, 1953, the body of Father W. Howard Bishop lay in state in Glenmary's Chapel. The fresh green leaves of late spring burst from every branch of the trees and shrubs around the mother house. In the pews sat the youth of Glenmary, serious young priests, Brothers and Sisters, brought to a realization of their own maturity and the flowering of their Society by the quiet figure, in priestly garb, lying there in his open coffin. From the Hierarchy came letters and telegrams of condolence. The Most Reverend Richard J. Cushing, Archbishop of Boston, wrote: "He was one of the country's best. I always looked upon him as a man especially chosen by God; simple, humble, full of faith and love for souls."

The Most Reverend Michael J. Ready, Bishop of Columbus, said: "He had the vision of a great priest and the constancy of a martyr."

His Eminence, Joseph Cardinal Pizzardo, wired from Rome: "When one looks at his death with the eyes of faith there is great cause for rejoicing, because this holy zealous priest of God — who had given his life strength to the cause of souls for the glory of God — was called while on duty. One could not wish for a more beautiful passage from this mortal life."

Monsignor Ligutti, the Executive Director of the National Catholic Rural Life Conference wrote: "Father Bishop was a great priest and a great man. His interest, his leadership, his earnestness in the work of Rural Life set many of us on fire. It was he who almost single-handed kept the flame of our organization alive. He sought out the practical fulfillment of our common ideals and hopes and he succeeded."

It was fitting that the Most Reverend George J. Rehring, Bishop of Toledo, who had known him intimately in life, should deliver his eulogy. He said in part:

"Regardless of the acclaim a priest may receive, he is a success only if he has worked for the glory of Christ. Father Bishop gave his life — his sixty-eight years — to the Church, to the Head and members of the Mystical Body.

"It was almost sixteen years ago that Father Bishop came to Cincinnati, with nothing but a holy ambition to found a Society for the conversion of Rural America. He was alone, without fellow workers and without material resources. He had come from his native Baltimore where he had a vision and a dream. During the years of his pastoral labors he had stared out into the wide open spaces of our beloved country and viewed with alarm the numerous counties in the states that were priestless. He was filled with a sense of deep responsibility to use his talent for the glory of his Creator and nothing could sway him to depart from the work he felt that in the Providence of God he was chosen to do.

"The beginnings were slow. Hopes for eventual success were counter-balanced by disappointments and reversals. Almost imperceptibly the Glenmary Missioners grew and expanded under the supervision of Archbishop McNicholas. Finally, approval was gained for the Society of Glenmary. In 1952 Archbishop Alter erected the Glenmary Religious Women as a Diocesan

Institute. In the meantime, active missionary labors were undertaken with success in the Dioceses of Cincinnati, Columbus, Wheeling, Owensboro, Savannah-Atlanta, and Tulsa-Oklahoma. Father Bishop had the satisfaction of seeing his work firmly grounded and holding promise of a glorious future.

"Today, the Glenmary Missioners have lost their Father-general, their founder and inspiration, but they have not lost their vocations as missioners, nor have they lost the leadership of Him who is the Head of the Mystical Body, nor have they lost the support of their fellow members in that Mystical Body.

"By working together as they have done in the past, motivated by a love for every human creature for the love of God, they will hasten the day when Glenmary will fulfill the dream and hope of its dynamic founder, whose memory must continue to fire them with zeal, and whose prayerful intercession before the throne of God will follow them in their labors."

So Father Bishop died, in death as in life, a valiant man of God. He was buried in Glenmary's own cemetery. His sons in the Society never fail to pray that they may have the same courage and the same success.

INDEX OF NAMES

117